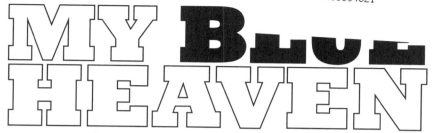

by Dante Friend
Foreword by John Stapleton

First published in 2004

EMPIRE PUBLICATIONS
1 Newton Street, Manchester M1 1HW
© Dante Friend 2004

ISBN 1 901 746 38 0

Cover design and layout: Ashley Shaw
Edited by: Ashley Shaw & Stuart Fish
Photographs: © Sporting Heroes Collection Ltd, Nick Wilkinson.
Printed in Great Britain by
Ashford Colour Press,
Gosport, Hants.

FOR MUM, DAD AND CARMEL.
ALL MY LOVE.

INTRODUCTION

Well I always felt I had a good book in me somewhere and as the two things that have taken over my life to an unhealthy extent have been writing and Manchester City, well I suppose something productive eventually had to happen.

So here it is - *My Blue Heaven*. Only it's not my Blue Heaven, rather it's the heaven of those legends who have performed so well for the club over the years. It's the games in which they played in that still give them goose pimples.

Rather than go for some of the more obvious names - I decided to speak to those who were City through and through and all immensely popular with the supporters. They can be put into three main categories. Local heroes, unsung heroes and cult heroes. Some, like Tommy Booth, are all three!

There are outstanding goalkeepers, resolute defenders, no-nonsense midfielders and fine attackers. There's the steady eddies and the skilful playmakers. Some of them we've heard from before in other books, while others haven't been fully recognised for their sterling efforts and perhaps they deserve their place in the sun also.

A special mention also to Neil Young who did so much for the club and who scored so many vital goals for us. Although he felt this wasn't the right time to tell his story, he did write me a lovely letter wishing me all the best with the book, which I thought fantastic.

A lot of this book was very easy for me. I mean, what can be better than having a series of conversations with some of the finest players to have ever worn a

Manchester City shirt. There are some good stories and some funny anecdotes and I've done my best to include a wide variety of players. There are the greats of the 60s and 70s, but also some unsung heroes of the 50s and cult heroes of the 80s and 90s an era when success seemed such along way away for City – yet the infrequent moments of joy shouldn't be forgotten either.

Maine Road has been and gone now and although it breaks my heart to see it being demolished (I still think there should have been some solution to keep it standing) my own personal blue heaven was simply going along each week, firstly in The Main Stand with my dad, later on in the Kippax with my friends and then finally in The North Stand. Being part of that magical place, the sights, the sounds, the funny chants and the heartbreaking moments is a part of my life that I can never forget.

I hope you all enjoy reading about the City stars and the day when they reached own personal blue heaven as much as I have writing about it.

Dante Friend
JANUARY 2004

ACKNOWLEDGEMENTS

On a personal note I'd like to place on record my sincere thanks to all the following people for their help in the production of this book.

John, Stuart, Ashley and all the team at *Empire Publications*, Clive Allen, Ken Barnes, Peter Barnes, Ian Bishop, Tommy Booth, Andy Buckley, Dave Cash, Bill Campbell, Ian Cheeseman, Paddy Fagan, Dave Goodstadt, Phill Gatenby, Dave Haslam, Paul Hince, Neil Harvey, Paul Lake, Mark Lillis, Roy Little, Rodney Marsh, Phil Noble, Alan Oakes, Steve Potter, Paul Power, Ian Penney, Kevin Roberts, Uwe Rosler, John Stapleton, Simon Thompson, Alex Williams, Nick Wilkinson, Brian Wilkinson, Dave Wallace, Gavin Westmoreland, Steve Wyeth, Paul Walsh, David White and Clive Wilson.

I also used the following publications and videos for research *Bleak and Blue*, Craig Winstanley; *Football With A Smile*, Gary James; *Soccer Legends - Bell, Lee, Summerbee* - BBC Video; *Manchester City - Moments To Remember*, John Creighton; *Blue And True*, Roddy Forsyth; *Manchester -The Greatest City* - Gary James.

CONTENTS

FOREWORD - JOHN STAPLETON
9TH DECEMBER 1967
FIRST DIVISION
CITY 4 TOTTENHAM HOTSPUR 1
ATT: 35,792

I first entered my Blue Heaven aged seven when my dad took me to Maine Road on the bus from Piccadilly. To the best of my recollection - it was a long time ago - City were playing Blackpool who had Stanley Matthews on the wing.

I sat on the wall of one of the tunnels through which spectators walked to take their place on the terraces. Just like my dad had done, just as my granddad had done when he watched the first ever game there in 1923.

These days my son Nick sits in the stands with me - the fourth generation of Blue Stapletons and just as passionate, just as much a City nut as any of us.

I grew up watching the 1955 and 1956 Cup Final teams with Bert Trautmann, Don Revie, Bobby Johnstone and my own personal hero Dave Ewing.

We lived in Saddleworth and I recall standing by the railway line for hours on a day they were playing Huddersfield in the hope that I might catch a glimpse of the team as they whistled by.

People like Paddy Fagan and Ken Barnes, both of whom contribute to this excellent book, are both people I am proud to count among my City old boys' network of mates.

Then, of course came the golden years under the wonderful Joe Mercer whose lovely widow Norah I still see from time to time. Years reflected in this book by that old powerhouse Alan Oakes who, with his cousin Glyn Pardoe, Mike Summerbee, Francis Lee and Colin Bell gave us some of the most breathtaking football we have ever seen.

My own favourite? Well it has to be the famous 'Ballet on Ice'. Regrettably, I was working in London that day but caught up with the Blues on *Match of the Day*.

A game in which they reigned so supreme that having hammered Spurs 4-1 with a goal of the decade from the under-rated Neil Young, Jimmy Greaves clapped them off the pitch and even Kenneth Wolstenholme seemed lost for words.

This book, with its recollections from stars spanning nearly fifty years of City triumphs, will evoke wonderful memories for all generations.

Enjoy it. I know I will.

John Stapleton
JANUARY 2004

ALAN OAKES
15TH APRIL 1970
EUROPEAN CUP WINNERS' CUP
SEMI-FINAL SECOND LEG
CITY 5 SCHALKE 04 1
ATT: 46,361

When people talk about the great Manchester City side of the late 60s and early 70s, the Holy Trinity of Bell, Lee and Summerbee is repeated *ad nauseam*. There will also be mention made of the likes of Neil Young, Mike Doyle, Tony Coleman, Joe Corrigan - magnificent servants whose contribution to the club has been recognised over the years.

However, in my humble opinion, the name Alan Oakes often gets overlooked and I wonder if it is because Oaky himself has never sought the limelight. He wasn't a forward who made headlines each week nor was he the main goal-supplier for that ace forward line but if we look carefully at the facts, few can doubt that Alan Oakes was one of the finest players ever to have graced the sky blue shirt.

Alan Oakes is the club's most decorated player. That is fact. No one has won more honours for City than Alan Oakes. Also fact is that no one has played more games for City than Oakes - 669 in all competitions, 565 of them in the league. His career spanned City's most successful era - he spent 17 glorious years in the first team, making his debut alongside the great Bert Trautmann and ending his career as the senior pro in 1976, alongside 'kids' such as Paul Power and Ged Keegan.

Alan Oakes was Mr Consistency. He wouldn't have stayed at the top for so long if he hadn't been. Alan Oakes is Manchester City through and through. He's delighted the team are making headlines for all the right reasons under Kevin Keegan - he also hopes someone goes on to surpass his records.

1

The trouble is that Alan played in so many of the club's greatest victories that, when he begins to pick out the highlights, it is hard to know where to start! So, we'll cover them all, through the eyes of a true legend and, for the record, a gentleman.

I put it to Alan that not just a team but a whole era was built around him. After all, his career spanned

the Les McDowall and Tony Book eras, "Well, yes I am very proud that I was there at the start and at the end," he replies with typical modesty. "I've got some wonderful memories and no-one can take them away from me, but records are there to be broken, aren't they? So if someone does take my record then all well and good. Although they play fewer league games than we did back then so they'd have to go some to pass it.

"I could never have foreseen when we were relegated in 1963, that we would bounce back as strongly as we did. We'd tried Les McDowall and George Poyser but when Joe and Malcolm arrived we just hit completely new heights and the influence that Malcolm in particular had on my career was amazing."

Alan Oakes remains a very modest man. He doesn't seem fazed by anything - which probably helped him perform in those key games back then. Whilst the others took all the acclaim, Alan went about his business with his usual efficiency and aplomb. He was the model professional, training hard and looking after his body, but most of all he had the talent within him to achieve the most glittering career the club has even seen.

Born in the sleepy Cheshire village

of Winsford on 7th September 1942, Oakes was a talented youngster who captained Cheshire Boys. A City fan from a young age, he came through the ranks at Maine Road and was thrown into the fray against Chelsea in November 1959. It is perhaps worth taking a look at the City side that took the field that day and earned a share of the spoils in a 1-1 draw. City lined up: Trautmann; Leivers, Sear; Cheetham, McTavish, Oakes; Barlow, Hayes, Hannah, Dyson and Colbridge.

So what was it like to make his debut alongside Bert Trautmann? Was he better than Frank Swift? "Well, first of all, I know I'm old but I'm not that old!" laughs Alan. "Seriously, I never saw Swifty play so I can't compare the two. But Bert was a legend. He was the experienced one then and I fancy he had a few calming words for me before we went out. I'd just signed from apprentice and although we looked up to him - we just accepted him. He didn't want to be the centre of attention, he never wanted to be treated any differently from anyone else, he just wanted to fit in. So although I respected him, after a while, I wasn't in awe of him, I just played alongside him."

Indeed, Jackie Dyson, Bill Leivers and Joey Hayes together with Bert were all heroes from Alan's early career. There was also, in the early 60s, a batch of youngsters breaking through who would eventually become household names. Mancunians Harry Dowd, Neil Young and Mike Doyle, and Alan's cousin from Winsford, Glyn Pardoe, who would be pitched in against Birmingham aged just 15 years and 314 days.

Unfortunately, it was the mid-60s

OPPOSITE:
City stalwart Oakes figured in the rebuilding of City under Mercer and Allison.

"I could never have foreseen when we were relegated in 1963, that we would bounce back as strongly as we did. We'd tried Les McDowall and George Poyser but when Joe and Malcolm arrived we just hit completely new heights and the influence that Malcolm in particular had on my career was amazing."

before these players really shone and things got worse for the club in the short term. Relegation finally came in 1963 and with it a three-year spell in the wilderness that was only broken when Joe and Malcolm came to shake things up. In the meantime Alan scored a cracking 30-yarder against Swindon Town before a mere 8,015 paying spectators at Maine Road - City's all-time lowest league attendance. If anything this proves Alan's commitment to the club - at their nadir the man went about his business in a determined and, on this occasion, spectacular fashion.

People remember the crowd but who talks about the goal? It was a trademark piledriver from Oakes, one of the 34 goals he scored for the club at an average of roughly two a year throughout his career. Although not a prolific goalscorer, Alan had a super shot on him and his natural engine meant he was the first name on the team sheet during the Mercer-Allison years, his game ideally suited to City's all-attacking, all-defending play.

The first seeds of recovery had been sown in the summer of 1965 when George Poyser made way for the late, great Joe Mercer OBE. Joe and Malcolm were to become major influences on Alan's career, helping him hit the heights during City's glory spell.

"The time that Malcolm spent with you on a one-to-one basis was a key ingredient. The fact that he listened and gave you his time made you feel enormously important and increased your confidence. He told us we were good players. He encouraged us. He was also very innovative, ahead of his time you know, and that gave us an advantage. We were very fit, he prepared us well physically and mentally."

City surged to promotion in 1966 and consolidated their position in the top flight the following season before, in 1967-68, City took the championship and Alan played his full part.

One of the early games that took the eye of the

watching millions on television was the 'ballet on ice', a 4-1 victory over Tottenham Hotspur in Arctic conditions at Maine Road. "As footballers you know if two or three of your team aren't playing well. Sometimes the team isn't at its best but you do enough to win the game. That game against Spurs though, and it was a fine Spurs side remember, I came off the pitch thinking 'wow, that was really something special to have been part of.' It's not very often that all 11 of you are on blob all at the same time and we also hit the bar a few times so it could have been even more."

To the surprise of most pundits and to the delight of most neutrals, City were lasting the distance in the title race. To fans starved of success whilst putting up with the numerous successes over in M16, City's 3-1 win at Old Trafford in March 1968 put the players firmly on the map. All of a sudden they were transformed from championship hopefuls to definite title contenders. However, instead of giving them the confidence to push on, the pressure seemed to get to a team who had never experienced such levels of expectation from the supporters before. After a couple of slip-ups Joe Mercer took City to Southport to recharge the batteries.

"The extra tension was getting to certain players and I remember Joe, who was never a ranter and a raver, ripped into us. He tore us to pieces and tried to get a reaction. He looked certain people in the eye and called them lazy, questioning their ambition. Well it certainly worked. Mike Summerbee squared up to Joe and rollocked the manager back! Joe just laughed at him, he'd got his reaction! He said, 'let's just get out there and win that league'.

"From then on we took the rest of the season by the scruff of the neck and we managed to nose in front by the time we went up to Newcastle. There was absolutely no consideration given to the game at Old Trafford because we all thought that United - playing at home - would beat lowly Sunderland - so from that point of view we knew exactly what we had to do... just win the game."

After that superb result in the derby the focus turned to the title run-in. City's form had slipped a little but after a 6-3 defeat at West Bromich Albion, United handed the initiative back to City when they beat Everton 2-0. It seemed no one wanted to win this league.

"We went down to Tottenham and gave a marvellous performance down there winning 3-1 and we all felt good about our chances on the Saturday."

The time had come. The final weekend of the season saw Manchester City face a tough assignment up at Newcastle whereas Manchester United entertained Sunderland at Old Trafford.

"Building up to the last game of the season - I repeat we were in a favourable position because we had nothing to lose, we were all just eager to get stuck in. We'd gone up on the Friday and stayed in our hotel up in Gateshead. We all had a dinner and some of us would get up and go for a walk, that sort of thing.

"On the Saturday morning I got up really early for breakfast. Normally we'd get up about 11.30am then walk it off a bit and then take the coach to the ground but on this particular morning I rose much, much earlier. I was trying to pass the time by simply talking about things - not the match though - everything and anything else! Time was going so slowly it was simply untrue. I just wanted to get started!

"Joe would never talk about the opposition team and didn't on this occasion either. Only about us. It was up to us how well we played, nothing else mattered. If we played to the best of our ability that was all that counted. You never worried about the opposition or composed tactics to counter a specific threat. I suppose that way we thought like a team, which helped us play like a team."

OPPOSITE:
City stalwart Alan Oakes is the most honoured player in the club's history and holder of the record number of appearances in a blue shirt.

City led 1-0 but were then pegged back to 1-1. City went 2-1 up but pegged it back to 2-2. In the second half they went 3-2 and then 4-2 up before a late Newcastle goal made it 4-3. Neil Young and Francis Lee were the heroes on the day but a season-long team effort was based on physical and mental strength together with selfless running and no little skill had won the day. It was a breathless afternoon. City were Champions of England for the first time since 1937 and although the Magpies had pegged City back on more than one occasion - Alan Oakes was never in any doubt that the league title was coming down the A1 with him.

"We weren't unduly worried about the opposition. We knew that if we let in 3 we could always score 4 and so it proved on this day. We had no idea what the score was in the United - Sunderland game and to be honest, we weren't interested. If we won, we were champions and that's all that counted. We did and we deserved it.

"There was a huge turn out from the City fans, 20,000 or so there and they were all mixed in with the home fans. Newcastle played well that day and gave us nothing. When Jackie Sinclair made it 2-2 with a superb volley to peg us back, we soon realised we'd have to roll our sleeves up and get in there even more. We had no indication of the scores elsewhere from management or supporters. To be honest - we didn't really want to know. We were pegged back to 4-3 but we kept on playing, we kept our heads. Then the final whistle blew - it was total joy and elation. We were champions. Joe and Malcolm and a lot of the players had been written off and for us to come back was very sweet indeed."

The curtain raiser to the following season was the Charity Shield, where City wiped the floor with West Brom 6-1. Amongst all the celebrations and well taken goals it's worth noting that in the case of the Albion goal, City were caught on the break after pushing right up on the visitors. The only player to get back and help the keeper was Alan Oakes who almost made a heroic clearance off the line. City were already cruising at 3-0 at this stage so it says something about his commitment that he made a lung-bursting 70 yard dash in a vain attempt to avert the goal.

1969 brought the FA Cup triumph against Leicester and victory at Wembley meant a return to European competition - a challenge Alan relished. He looks back on that ultimately successful Cup Winners' Cup run of 1969-70 with a lot of pride. It also gave him and the other City players the chance to bury the ghost of Fenerbahçe once and for all.

The run in the competition allowed the Blues to sample five European countries: Spain, Belgium, Portugal, Germany and Austria and as far as English supporters were concerned, transport to those destinations remained expensive and English clubs didn't enjoy the huge travelling support they do in European competitions today. Indeed, barely 5,000 City supporters were present for the final in Vienna's Prater stadium. Nevertheless, for the fans who had the money to travel to these exotic destinations, they must have enjoyed every single minute of an epic journey that would put Manchester City on the footballing map forever.

First out of the hat were Basque giants

"Fenerbahçe was a disaster for the club. For all of us. So we gained a huge amount of confidence from the Bilbao result. It was our springboard for success."

Athletic Bilbao, later of course managed by someone else with City connections, Howard Kendall, but at the time managed by another Englishman, Ronnie Allen. At least this ensured fair play and Corinthian spirit all round. "Against Fenerbahçe we were up against a hell of a lot of intimidation. From their players and from their fans. Bilbao away was no easy assignment and we were under no illusions when the draw was made. However, they were a good sporting team and they didn't resort to any foul play or petulance at all. A 3-3 draw away from home in Europe is a great result - whatever the opposition or the era. I'm not sure if away goals actually counted in those days but although we hadn't won, we felt they were there for the taking in the second leg. We were coming back to Maine Road with something to show for our efforts."

Alan took centre stage in the return scoring in a 3-0 win for City the club's first win in Europe at the fourth attempt. This triumph allowed the club to progress further with real purpose. In fact, from the sorry exit in Istanbul, City remained undefeated in Europe for nearly three years. It was only when a cruel streak of injuries ripped apart the heart of City's team before the 1971 ECWC semi-final against Chelsea that the blue juggernaut was halted. So, it is good to remember that a stunning strike from Alan Oakes in the game was the moment that finally lit the blue touch paper for the club in Europe.

"Fenerbahçe was a disaster for the club. For all of us. So we gained a huge amount of confidence from the Bilbao result. It was our springboard for success."

In the next round, Belgian outfit SK Lierse were brushed aside with consummate ease, thanks to a Colin Bell masterclass - an 8-0 aggregate victory that in all honesty could have been double that. Academica Coimbra provided the quarter-final opposition and the real obstacle here was not so much the quality of the Portuguese opposition but the intense heat and humidity of the Iberian weather.

During this time City were all guns blazing in the League Cup, having disposed of neighbours United in one of the most thrilling two-legged semi-finals ever. A 2-1 win at Maine Road followed by a 2-2 draw at Old Trafford. A tie Alan recalls fondly:

"If City met United in a semi-final these days, they hype surrounding the game would be out of this world, but we played each other a number of times and we had the edge over them. They say derbies are levellers and they were always keenly contested but from the night we won 3-1 at Old Trafford in 1968 we were clearly the better team. I think we came out on top because we had better players than United.

"The atmosphere in those two games though was brilliant. Of course Stepney touched the free kick and that made it legal to score from the rebound. That put us into the final. I was so pleased for my cousin Glyn Pardoe that he scored the winner in the League Cup Final at Wembley. It was nice for him to get some of the limelight. To be fair, the way we dug in that day and fought for everything was terrific. We deserved that result after what we'd been through that week.

"The thing that was so special about that week was we were playing in tropical conditions over there and Malcolm thought he'd do us all a favour by arranging for the club to stay overnight and acclimatise there. Now the Portuguese were a completely different proposition to anything we'd faced before. They were a good passing team, they kept the ball well and were a decent side. So we spent a lot of the time chasing the ball.

"The next day though, all our plans backfired because we were delayed by heavy snow for 13 hours on our return to England. Even then we had to divert to Gatwick or Birmingham possibly, I'm not sure which, so we had very little time to recuperate before Wembley and as you know, the final against West

Brom went to extra time, a further energy sapping 30 minutes on top of the normal 90 on a terrible pitch. As I say, this was the day that Glyn made his mark."

With the League Cup in the bag and the Portuguese out of the way, City strode confidently into the semi-finals. Which brings us to Alan's favourite night in a Manchester City shirt. It was the night City tore one of the best sides in Germany to pieces, a 5-1 thrashing of Schalke 04 that took City all the way to the Cup Winners' Cup Final in Vienna.

Although Alan didn't score in this game - he set up the first 3 goals. If you were fortunate enough to have been present on the night, you'll recall the score but the memory may have faded slightly by now. One look at the game on the Bell, Lee, Summerbee soccer legends video tells you all you need to know about Alan Oakes' performance that night - it was the performance of someone at the very top of his game.

"We respected the Germans, but we knew that full time over there was only half-time in the tie overall, so the only instruction was to make sure we were still in with a chance by the time we got back to Manchester. We lost 1-0 over there, which wasn't a disaster. We were relatively satisfied with that, because we knew we had something to fight for in the second leg."

Maine Road was expectant. Over 46,000 supporters packed into the famous old stadium. Schalke, hailing from the Ruhr Valley, were one of the biggest clubs in Germany. They had won a number of titles in the late 30s and early 40s prompting speculation that they received favours from the state and that they were the team Hitler supported!

"Sitting in the dressing room before the game, the players seemed to be generally relaxed. If there was any extra tension around, then I certainly wasn't aware of it. Joe just asked us to go out there and enjoy the game and savour the atmosphere. The crowd were there to support us and here was a chance to show everybody how well we could play. So the instruction was to simply enjoy it because you'll play better if you're relaxed than if you're uptight. Play well. Attack them and get the goals."

Get the goals is just what City did in a blistering start at Maine Road. Oakes set up the first *three* goals of the game, with unbelievable pinpoint cross-field balls into the paths of Mike Doyle once and Neil Young twice. There followed spectacular strikes: Doyley's shot cannoned in off the crossbar nearly took the roof off Maine Road.

Meanwhile, Alan was taking pot shots at the Schalke goalie all night and his midfield display battered the Germans into submission. "Like I say, we were an all-attacking, all-defending team. That's how they wanted us to play and although my role was more defensive than Mike Doyle, when you had the ball you pushed on and looked to play someone in and when they had it you dropped back and got men behind the ball. I was a box-to-box player at times. There was no frustration on my part that I wasn't a star man or anything. After the horrors of relegation I was content to stay in the team, I was happy and delighted that the club was doing so well and that I was a part of that. I had to fight for my place at times but I believe I lasted so long because of the coaching and mentoring from the likes of Malcolm Allison. Pulling me to one side, talking through situations, giving me the chance to give my opinion. On top of all that I was very physically fit. I didn't go out on the town like some players - the bright lights of Manchester never really appealed to me."

From there City moved onto the pouring rain in Vienna where Gornik of Poland were despatched 2-1 with goals from Young and Lee. The European Cup Winners' Cup joined the League Cup, the FA Cup, League Championship, Second Division Championship and the Charity shield in the trophy cabinet.

City were to go close in the League and lose in Wembley finals and the Charity Shield over the next few seasons - they were still a good team, but they somehow failed to win anything. It coincided with the arrival of Rodney Marsh.

"Well first time round there could be no doubting that Malcolm was the man at City. Second time round obviously things went horribly wrong. I think he always fancied himself as a bit of a manager and I think he pushed Joe into the Marsh signature. That's how I saw it. Later on, it was such a shame that the partnership that had achieved so much for City was allowed to break up and the politics upstairs in the club started to infiltrate to that level. He was burning with ambition, Malcolm, but at the time, it is fair to say that Rodney didn't fit into the team pattern and that cost us the league. If he was going to buy Rodney, he should've just left him on the bench and kept the original XI for the rest of the season. If we were losing or struggling, then bring him on, see if he wins you the game. Rodney Marsh was a fantastic player, but that way we could have had the best of both worlds."

1974 was a bittersweet year as City lost to Wolves in the League Cup final. That season had seen the return of Denis Law and what a return it turned out to be. "Denis came back and of course he scored the goal, the backheel, which sent United down. Obviously people like Doyley saw it one way - he was slapping Denis on the back in the dressing room but Denis was distraught, but for me and most of the City players that day, we saw it a bit differently.

"We just went there to do a job. The derbies are for the fans. You want to win for those people that come to support you, so it was great to see the City fans celebrating - before it all went off in the ground - but I say again I had nothing personal against the United players. I wished no ill to Manchester United. I didn't particularly want to see them relegated. If City can finish first and United second every year that would do for me. I maintain though, we were the better team in our games with United, the results speak for themselves."

The 1976 League Cup run gave Alan the chance to enjoy one last hurrah, a final swansong in front of the twin towers. Alan was now the father figure who helped bring on the younger members of that cup side.

He fired a goal in against Mansfield Town in round five and then scored the crucial second with a trademark 30 yarder during the 4-0 semi-final demolition of Middlesbrough. He played his part in the never-to-be-forgotten derby of November 1975 when City battered United 4-0, on the night Colin Bell was stretchered off following a horrendous and, in the eyes of City supporters, vicious challenge, from fiery Scot Martin Buchan. All of which meant a final Wembley appearance for Alan and a chance to bow out at the top. City's 2-1 win over Newcastle proved to be their last major triumph.

"You wouldn't have thought it possible that a club, an institution, like City would have gone so long without a major honour but that's football I suppose. The finances these days have gone crazy and I hate it when I turn on the telly and I see them feigning injury and rolling over! What's the matter with them!

"I think City are doing fantastically well under Kevin Keegan but for me, the most important thing is to stay in that Premier League at all costs. We know what it's like outside the Premiership and it's not nice. I was awfully sad to leave Maine Road because of the wonderful memories it held for me personally. They were an absolutely brilliant set of lads, on and off the pitch; Belly, Mike, Tony Book, Franny, Doyley, Youngy... but I understand the club must progress and if this helps us attract a new generation of superstars then so be it. With a bit of luck, a new golden era will soon be here for Manchester City."

ALEX WILLIAMS
11TH MAY 1985
SECOND DIVISION
CITY 5 CHARLTON 1
ATT: 47,285

Alex Williams is eating a hot and very tasty looking kebab. It's lunchtime in the City In The Community office and Alex is tucking in. "I've had to send someone out to get it for me," he chuckles. Ah yes, we're in the new stadium now and there aren't the same number of takeaways and restaurants as there are on Wilmslow Road! It's another reminder that to so many people Maine Road and its surrounding area was home. And as someone who was born and brought up in Moss Side, the move to Eastlands has affected Alex more than most - and not just in terms of trying to get a lunchtime kebab! But he's all for progress.

"I was always a City fan," says Alex, "there was a group of us who would often go and watch both teams, City and United on alternate Saturdays. That doesn't happen these days but back then it was quite common. I can honestly say I never really felt the same buzz when United scored as when City scored. I was watching great players like Rodney Marsh and it was great entertainment in those days.

"I was spotted playing at school level by John Collins, the City scout, who sadly passed away only recently. I'd started off playing junior Sunday League and soon I became a regular for Manchester boys. When I went along for training at City it was under the guidance of Steve Fleet, the former City keeper. When I was an amateur I'd be learning off brilliant people like Joe Corrigan and Keith MacRae. Unfortunately I was just too young to feature in the 1978 Central League winning side, but to have clinched the title obviously showed the depth of talent we had in the City squad then.

"Also, there were a lot of Manchester lads in the reserves and in the youth team at City and right through my time in the first team we had a good record of bringing through good local talent. I went to the same school as Roger Palmer, although he was a few years older than me, so we weren't big mates or anything like that, but when I arrived at City he was already there and so we struck up an understanding, as we'd been aware of each other being footballers even though our paths hadn't crossed up until then.

"Other local lads I was great friends with were Gary and Dave Bennett, from Rusholme, good footballers the Bennett brothers, Clive Wilson, from Greenheys, another one with great creative ability, there was Gary Buckley from Salford, a good lad who was thrown into the deep end in a really big game early in his career, I think it was Liverpool in the League Cup semi and much later on Eric Nixon, a cracking keeper who'd previously been at Curzon Ashton.

"I could see all these players making a breakthrough and it encouraged me to keep plugging away, to stay focused and go all the way with City too. By the time I was leaving school I'd made the England youth set-up and I knew I was signing forms with Manchester City. They had a big vote at Wilbraham High school to see who had the best career in front of them and guess what - I won! Being prospective goalkeeper for Manchester City won me the competition!"

By the turn of the decade Malcolm Allison had returned and there was a definite lack of stability in the air although Alex was bedding in nicely at Maine Road. He was, at that age, a bundle of enthusiasm as well as being blessed with more than his fair share of talent. It is at this stage of his fledgling career that Alex was part of City's youth cup team - which also presented Alex with his first real experience of racism in the raw. Sadly, it wasn't to be his last.

"I remember playing down at Millwall. We drew 0-0 but the stick I got was unbelievable. Certain grounds never seem to change: Millwall, Leeds, Chelsea. At Stamford Bridge in the League Cup I got a lot of abuse. Things are different these days although I have to say I feel people are still racist and there are elements in society that haven't gone away - but it is better. When you look at the progress we've made in this country and compare it to places like Italy and Germany then you can see in Europe they've still got someway to go to stamp it out. When I played on loan at Queen of the South the fans were racist too, but their problem with me wasn't that I was black, it was because I was English!"

Alex finally made his debut in 1981. It was a proud moment for the Mancunian. "I had a little inkling during the week that I'd be playing on the Saturday against West Brom as Joe Corrigan was carrying an injury. On the Saturday morning I was told to report to the ground and as soon I arrived they told me I was in the starting XI. Maybe they had left it to the day of the match so that I wouldn't have the chance to get too nervous. As soon as I knew I phoned all my family and friends. As it turned out only my dad could make it that afternoon, in spite of that it was truly great day for me, we won 2-1 and they only scored a consolation goal in the last few minutes.

"Bobby McDonald put us in front with a header, from a corner flicked on by Caton and that was followed up by a Tueart goal just before half-time. I had the odd save to make but to be honest West Brom didn't look too threatening even though they featured City old boys Gary Owen and Peter Barnes among their number.

"It was Bryan Robson who scored their late consolation. I remember early on they had a shot and I tipped one over the bar. It wasn't a particularly difficult save to make but it was nice to get that early touch, just to settle me down."

Alex was still very much an understudy to Big Joe at this point but now and again he'd get a run in the first team and always performed with great distinction whenever called upon. One of his best games was in City's 2-1 win at Tottenham in 1982. Although Graham Baker's double secured the points, it was a one-man show of brilliance from young Williams that catapulted him to the attention of the national media. Later, in the spring of 1983, Corrigan departed.

"Joe was off to Seattle and I had heard on the grapevine that City were looking for an experienced replacement, with Pat Jennings' name mentioned. Nothing ever materialised and I was handed the No 1 jersey. Finances were tight at the time at City, however I'd like to think John Benson had enough faith in me to give me the shirt on merit."

Alex proved a safe pair of hands but a confidence crisis and an injury plague decimated City's season. Liverpool came to Maine Road and won 4-0 but Williams actually had a great game. At Stoke, lady luck deserted the Blues when Paul Power unluckily had a goal chalked off for offside. City were huffing and puffing with all their might but the teams below them were catching up. Victory over West Ham was followed by defeats against Arsenal and Nottingham Forest. In the penultimate match of the season, City headed south to the Goldstone Ground. "I remember us going down to Brighton and winning 1-0 thanks to a Kevin Reeves goal. We were all celebrating on the pitch at the end as we thought we'd done enough. Brighton and Swansea were down but as it turned out we still needed a point against Luton on the Saturday."

Luton lost 3-0 at Old Trafford in midweek which meant the situation was unchanged by the Saturday morning of the match. A draw would be good enough to preserve City's status.

"I suppose the big difference between the Luton game and the Charlton game was that in '83 there was a negative tension, but in '85 there was a positive tension. The fans expected us to win on both occasions but the longer the game went on against Luton the more the tension about the place became unbearable. A couple of players maybe weren't showing for the ball on the day... alright, we weren't creating a lot but time was ticking down - albeit slowly. I punched the ball out for the Antic goal but the ball got stuck and we didn't clear it properly. Antic whacked it and it deflected off a defender past me as I was standing up. It wasn't my fault for the goal, it was a collective thing at the back, but gasps and then silence greeted it and it was a terrible moment in the dressing room afterwards. It was absolutely horrendous, for me both as a City player and as a City fan."

The ultimate had happened. City would be playing in the Second Division for the first time since 1966. A proud record had gone and supporters were looking to the future. "1983-84 was a tough season. The attitude of the fans was that we were going up and it wasn't going to be a problem."

In fact, City's problem was that they lost at home to

OPPOSITE: Alex's performances in the wake of Joe Corrigan's departure led at least one Fleet Street journalist to claim that he would win more England caps than his illustrious predecessor

the three sides that finished directly above them that season... Chelsea, Sheffield Wednesday and a Keegan-inspired Newcastle all took three points off the Blues and City's failure to seal automatic promotion did nothing to ease their financial plight.

OPPOSITE:
A tireless trainer, Alex's career was cut cruelly short by injury. Still a young man, he retired in 1988 following a spinal injury.

"Billy McNeill came in and put the team together for a song really. A lot of Scottish lads - Jim Tolmie, Derek Parlane, Gordon Smith, Gordon Dalziel - we'd have a 5-a-side game in training, England v Scotland, and sometimes we'd struggle to put an England team out. We did have some good players there though and later on we added some even better ones in the shape of Mark Lillis, David Phillips and Neil McNab."

An ever present in 1983-84, Alex also played in every game in the promotion season 1984-85. His contribution was to prove vital during a campaign that never really got into full flow until the late autumn. A Steve Kinsey strike saw off leaders Oxford and a David Phillips goal saw off Birmingham City. Those two teams would ultimately finish above City that season but it showed that The Blues weren't out of their depth at the summit of the Second Division.

As the season reached its thrilling climax, City had a couple of opportunities to put the promotion issue beyond all doubt. After a glorious win at rivals Portsmouth, a nervy goalless draw with neighbours Oldham Athletic was then followed by horror show at Meadow Lane, where upwards of 12,000 Blues massed in the Spion Kop expecting the team to wrap up promotion. A 3-2 defeat meant the City supporters did not remain in party mood. "I remember that day well. We were 3-0 down at half-time and the City fans were going absolutely beserk inside the ground. We got it together a bit after the break but the damage had already been done and we had to go to the final week. Like I say, there was pressure associated with the Charlton game but it was a different type of pressure. The way we did it, a last day drama, was City all over.

A bit like the Gillingham game in as much as only City could drag things out to the last game of the season."

City had a number of problems in the build up to the game. Nicky Reid and Mick McCarthy were suspended and the dreaded injury curse had afflicted the club again with Clive Wilson, Graham Baker and Gordon Smith all unavailable for selection.

"Charlton weren't without injury problems either," said Alex, "Bob Bolder, their very good experienced keeper, was out that day so they had a 17-year-old youngster playing called Lee Harmsworth. Maybe the occasion got to him, maybe he had a bit of stage fright because he was certainly indecisive and I think that resulted in a couple of our goals that day. He seemed reluctant to come off his line."

In truth, City were never in danger that day. Especially when David Phillips scored the first and when Andy May placed a delicious header just under the crossbar for 2-0 there was absolute pandemonium on the Kippax. This was the breathing space City needed. This was the day City were going up.

"The team talk had been very simple. It was just go out and win the game. At half time we sat down knowing we were half way there, but we felt relatively sure that Charlton weren't going to trouble us enough to get back into the game. They weren't showing

much and the orders were just to keep it tight for the first 15 minutes of the second half and the rest would look after itself."

In actual fact, before anyone knew it City were 5-0 up. Jim Melrose, carrying a knock, looped a header over the hapless Harmsworth and then Paul Simpson, who had been so influential in the run-in, rounded him to make it four. David Phillips then produced his usual blockbuster, straight out of the top drawer for number five, a goal that nearly took the net off the posts at the Platt Lane end as well as the roof off the Kippax stand itself. This was unbridled joy and the City fans drank it all in. With half an hour to go and promotion assured, fans and players had the chance to enjoy the rest of the game with no pressure on their shoulders at all.

A young Robert Lee scored for Charlton, a goal that drew ironic cheers from the City fans. A massive pitch invasion ensued at full time and the players took the salute from the directors' box.

"It felt good to clinch promotion. For me it wasn't about avenging the Luton game or anything like that because as I said earlier, I didn't feel I was particularly to blame for that goal or for relegation. I was thrown into the fray late on that year, but to get the club back where it belonged, in front of nearly 50,000 of our supporters, well it was fantastic. We had a brilliant party afterwards down at Mere Golf and Country club, I think that was something to do with the late Stephen Boler but the atmosphere among the lads was amazing. I felt our promotion had been fully deserved. I kept 22 clean sheets that season and I was delighted with that."

1985-86 saw a few early wins before a

> **"For me it wasn't about avenging the Luton game... because I didn't feel I was particularly to blame for that goal or for relegation. I was thrown into the fray late on that year, but to get the club back where it belonged, in front of nearly 50,000 of our supporters, well it was fantastic.**

ᴀʟᴇx WILLIAMS

3-0 derby defeat that turned out to be Alex Williams' swansong in goal for Manchester City. A recurrence of an old back injury meant that just after he'd worked so hard to get the club back in the big time, the promising keeper was deprived of fulfilling his true potential at the age and level where he'd be firmly in the spotlight.

"I have no regrets these days. I'm still involved with the club I love and I can do things that really make a difference. I sometimes think if I'd been a player 10 years later I'd be a millionaire by now. But then again, I played 120 odd games for Manchester City, the team I love, and I'm happy and healthy. Compared to poor Tommy Caton and Marc Vivien Foe, the fact I didn't play on means nothing really. Fate's been kind to me in comparison."

CLIVE **ALLEN**
6TH OCTOBER 1991
FIRST DIVISION
NOTTS COUNTY 1 CITY 3
ATT 11,878

City have often been unlucky when choosing star strikers. The big name, big money purchases that set fans' hopes soaring have often ended in disappointment, bewilderment and a reiteration of that old chestnut 'the City curse'. For example, the arrival of Rodney Marsh back in 1972 was supposed to ensure a second title for the Mercer-Allison management team. Yet Marsh into City didn't go and league form slipped, although Rodney remains highly regarded by City supporters, his spell at the club left supporters wondering what might have been.

Then there was Mick Channon, the free-scoring England and Southampton centre-forward, who was supposed to be the final piece in the jigsaw in 1977. Yet after a reasonable start his form and that of the team slipped alarmingly and a couple of years later Channon returned to The Dell where he resumed his goalscoring exploits.

John Bond's acquisition of Million Pound Man Trevor Francis in 1981 sent the City supporters wild with delight. They massed in their thousands at the old Victoria Ground as Francis scored twice on his debut in a 3-1 win at Stoke. A superb turn and shot from 30 yards on Boxing Day that year against Wolves briefly put City top of the League but Francis suffered numerous injuries while he was at the club and as a consequence didn't enjoy a consistent run in the side, although his goals to game ratio was still outstanding. Before we knew it though, Francis had been sold to Sampdoria by Peter Swales and the rot had set in with John Bond departing months afterwards. For some reason Francis' career seemed blighted at Maine Road and City fans saw less than the best from their new hero.

Even among the lesser lights, the likes of Paul Stewart for example, who was idolised by the City faithful in 1987-88 when he found the net 28 times, the club has faced disappointment. His departure to Tottenham left many fans upset that they never saw Paul Stewart go all the way in sky blue.

All of which brings us to Clive Allen. When Mel Machin laid out £1.1 million in August 1989 to secure his services from Bordeaux, the City support was absolutely ecstatic. It seemed a monumental signing. Allen had some pedigree. A member of the entertaining Tottenham side of the mid-80s, Allen had notched 49 goals in 1986-87 and to many Spurs fans had finally filled the scoring boots of their great striker Jimmy Greaves.

Allen was also ecstatic at the move. It was to be his only northern club in a career based almost entirely in the capital. Arsenal (briefly), Crystal Palace, QPR, Tottenham, Millwall, Chelsea and West Ham all benefited from the striking prowess of Stepney born Clive, one of the famous trio of Allen brothers, the others being of course Martin and Bradley.

Yet Clive's career at City was derailed by injury and a fall-out of astronomical proportions with manager Peter Reid precipitated a premature exit from Maine Road. Yet Clive is still revered by the City faithful and it's a mutual respect according to Allen, as they helped him come to terms with a lonely ten-week spell on the sidelines. There were some fleeting moments of happiness and there was one afternoon when the player and his fan club celebrated together in sheer delight, as Clive recalls, "There's only one game I can choose for my favourite during my time at City, the Notts County game where I scored 2 goals."

One thing people might not have known is that Clive could have been on City's books much earlier. "When I heard that City had come in for me I was over the moon. Really and truthfully. I'd had a trial up at City as a 15-year-old schoolboy and I got injured in a practice match. Roy Bailey gave me some treatment and some good advice and Ken Barnes also spent some time with me talking about things and giving me some tremendous advice. I always had good vibes about the place. I'd always wondered if I'd go back at some stage and here was my chance. When I returned Roy Bailey was still there and it was nice to see his face again.

"The club had just been promoted and Mel Machin told us what he expected us to do over the next few years. He was very excited. I was just delighted because there had been some financial irregularities at Bordeaux at the time and the chairman was in all sorts of trouble. Players were leaving left, right and centre and the whole thing was falling apart."

Clive joined a forward line that boasted both Trevor Morley and David Oldfield but to the supporters he was the number one forward on our books. Here was a class 'A' striker, a player with real pedigree who'd scored 49 goals in one season for Tottenham Hotspur, a record that meant he could probably have his pick of any club in Europe... and here he was lining up for Manchester City.

Allen took some time to find the net, but when he did for the first time, in his fifth game, his turn and snapshot at the North Stand end proved to be the winner against his old club QPR. Shortly after that the injury jinx began.

OPPOSITE:
Clive's genius as a striker made him an instant hit at Maine Road - his strike rate of a goal every two games should have been enough to secure a regular first team place...

"Sometimes I'm talking with people about football and someone will always say, 'you were at City when they beat United 5-1, what was that like to play in? It must have been brilliant...' but I'd picked up an Achilles injury beforehand and still not recovered. As it was, I attended my sister-in-law's wedding down south that day. Can you believe it, the wedding took place at 3pm on Saturday 23rd September!

"Obviously everyone had an interest in the score and after 20 or 30 minutes City were two or three goals up and no-one could believe it. I couldn't believe I was missing out on such a day! I'd loved to have played but it just wasn't to be. I did fear for my place in the side because the lads who played that day did so well."

When he returned to the side it was in some style. Picture the scene, 90 minutes gone and City, without a point all season away from home, are 1-0 down to Chelsea in a really poor game. The travelling army again wondering why on earth they bothered to make the long journey. Then came a moment that makes you drop your chicken balti pie. A moment those who were there would never forget.

"I just remember we were playing stoppage time and I was quite deep, the ball came to me just about five or ten yards or so into the Chelsea half. I was on the right hand side and took it on the bounce first touch - and whack - it sailed right into the net from 40 yards! Chelsea felt aggrieved because there was some dispute over a throw-in or something. Well it was a special moment and you don't get many goals like that in your career."

As Clive struggled to regain fitness and form, City's overall league position meant the end of the road for Mel Machin and in his place came the former Everton manager Howard Kendall.

"I got on well with Howard and still do. Although I didn't start every game under him, I was still made to feel part of the squad with Howard. Often I'd start, other times he'd bring me on for the last 30 minutes or so, but he'd explain my role and would also explain the reasons if I was omitted. That season he took over when we were bottom. By the end of the season we'd finished a respectable 14th and I'd scored 10 goals or so in 14 games.

"I developed a good relationship with Niall Quinn when he came in, to be honest we hit it off straight away. It's laughable that later on Peter Reid, a manager who wouldn't explain to you why you were omitted, cited his decision to transfer me as down to me not fitting in and not being someone who could play off Quinny. In this spell though and those later on, we were always scoring goals as a partnership and making goals for each other too."

Clive grabbed some vital goals towards the end of 1989-90. April saw City end their miserable away record with a win at Villa as the Blues finished the season on a high. The arrival of the Mighty Quinn had perked up everyone's spirits at the club and goal poacher Allen was able to put away the big Irishman's flick-ons.

1990-91 saw City's squad strengthened further and the prospect of a fully-fit Allen together with a City side fully consolidated in the top flight meant hopes were high of Allen regaining his magic touch.

28

Kendall started the season with Heath partnering Quinn but Clive still came off the bench to score some vital goals. Yet when Peter Reid took over, he remained on the bench. On many occasions he was supersub, but to the fans that saw his replacement score one league goal all season, the former England international, a man who had played in that famous 2-0 win over Brazil in The Maracana, was the man who could win us the league. To many, having Allen on the bench was a criminal waste of talent. Although not as quick as in his Spurs heyday, he still had match-winning qualities to offer.

Evidence of this came in the FA cup fourth round at Vale Park that season. The Blues had disposed of Burnley at Turf Moor in round three, former Blackburn man Colin Hendry endearing himself even further to the Clarets' supporters by scoring the only goal. At Vale Park, City led through Niall Quinn after 12 minutes but the Valiants equalised through former City man Darren Beckford on 36. John Rudge's outfit were a tough nut to crack and for long periods the tie was in the balance. Enter Clive Allen.

"The game was still 1-1 when I came on and we had a corner so before the ball was delivered I ran onto the field to great cheers from the City end. There was 20 minutes to go. I remember timing my run to perfection and as it came in, I'm sure there was a flick-on, and I nodded it in at the far post with my first touch! After the game City fans were telling me what a lucky charm I was, that our name was on the cup, that the goal was the stuff of legends. To be honest we had a great feeling about the cup that year. In the following round though, we did everything but score at Notts County. Their keeper saved everything

"I just remember we were playing stoppage time and I was quite deep, the ball came to me just about 5 or 10 yards or so into the Chelsea half. I was on the right hand side and took it on the bounce first touch - and whack - it sailed right into the net from 40 yards!"

and their last minute goal was a fluke."

Allen, who was to experience cup pain at Wembley with Tottenham and QPR, never got so far with City. His goal scoring record was undoubted. His ability unquestioned. His relationship with City's young manager was not so strong though.

"I don't know whether it was down to his inexperience as a manager but I should not have been treated the way I was by Peter Reid. I trained with the kids for ten weeks; Garry Flitcroft, Michael Hughes, Mike Sheron and all those who were there at the time - and all this because he wanted me to go and I wanted to stay and fight for my first team place. He never spoke to me in that time and he held it against me that I went against his wishes. There were some painful times, but after three or four weeks I just thought, 'what the hell, I'm going to tough it out and see it through. I can play for whoever I want!' The fans gave me support whenever they saw me. I didn't play a huge amount of games in the end for City but my goal ratio was one in two - I feel closer to them as a set of supporters than I do with any other club. I've still got a great rapport with them.

"That was the most unhappy I'd ever been in my career. I had a spell at Palace under Terry Venables when things weren't working out, but it just wasn't the right club for me. I felt City was the right club for me but the manager wouldn't even speak to me for weeks and weeks. Like I said before I wasn't really a Kendall type player but he at least made me feel wanted, part of the team. I didn't get any of that with Reidy.

"One afternoon, I think it was a Friday afternoon, I got a call from Sam Ellis saying I was to report to Maine Road on Saturday morning. I was in the squad for Notts County. There had been a huge injury crisis and I think Reidy had exhausted all the other avenues. I think he'd even have picked Jason Beckford or Ashley Ward or any of the kids before

me, but as there was no one else, I
was suddenly back in the frame. I
turned up for the get-together and
the banter was flying about, which
was great. Gary Megson turned
round and said, 'who's the new
player?' and everyone had a good
laugh.

"The media picked up quite
quickly on the situation and there
was quite a lot of hype regarding
my comeback. All the City fans
were packed into the Kop End
behind the goal and gave me such
a warm reception, I'll never forget
that."

Allen was a substitute and with the Blues struggling
to see off the Magpies with 20 minutes left, it was
down to Allen to save the day and win the game.
There was something in the air that day. It was as if
the script had been prepared for him. With his first
touch he produced a blistering shot that was handled
on the line. Penalty!

"We got the penalty and Stevie Redmond, I think,
was the penalty taker still at that stage although Reidy
took one at Leeds and missed and might've fancied it
again. Reddo picked up the ball and I was right next
to him. He just went, 'do you want to take it Clive?'
And I grabbed it off him and said 'Do I want to take
it? Indeed!'

"I remember when I saw it hit the back of the net
I'd never experienced such a feeling of relief and joy
all at the same time. I'd had to keep all that anger
and hurt to myself for ten long weeks, I'd kept my
dignified silence but I knew eventually, one way or
another, I'd have my say and I was having it now.

"Okay, I think everybody knows I'm not what you'd
call a Peter Reid player. However I felt I had a part to

play at that club and if it was commitment to that club and shirt he was looking forward, then he couldn't have faulted me on that score. I kissed my badge and ran over to the City fans and that was another magic moment.

"Literally 90 seconds after the restart I connected so sweetly with a cross from the right and buried a volley right into the bottom corner and I can tell you that goal meant so much to me. Again it was over to those City fans and by now I'd been on the field four minutes and I'd scored twice! People don't remember it was Mike Sheron's debut that day and he scored a good goal. We won the game 3-1 and we'd slipped up in a few games previously so obviously all the headlines were going to be about me getting even, but I was quite comfortable with that.

"After the game the press wanted a word and I told the world how I was answering my manager by doing the business on the pitch. I suppose it could have got me into further trouble and on the Monday he called to see me again. He said he was outraged by the stuff he'd read that morning and started laying into me again. I said, 'whatever, I don't care. You've done your worst now. What are you going to do? Put me back in with the kids. Go on, make me train with the kids again!' He said, 'No, you're playing at Stockport against Chester in the League Cup and we need you again for that.' Well we won on the Tuesday 3-0 and I scored once again. All the City fans chanted 'Are you watching Peter Reid?' and the media again seized on the situation, all of a sudden he was the one who was having to defend his position. He said, 'Clive does what he does best - score goals.' I suppose that was as much praise as I would ever get.

"I don't know whether it was down to his inexperience as a manager but I should not have been treated the way I was by Peter Reid. I trained with the kids for 10 weeks... because he wanted me to go and I wanted to stay and fight for my first team place."

He was telling the press that he'd always enjoyed a good relationship with the City fans and couldn't understand the barracking. He was in the spotlight now.

"Soon after I picked up a little injury again, which was a disaster for me because I felt it would have been exceptionally difficult for him to leave me out. That injury was another six-weeker and after that I knew my time at the club was numbered."

That Christmas, Allen was sold to Chelsea for £250,000, a staggering loss of £850,000 for a player who had scored 16 league goals in 31 starts. On New Year's Day 1992 Clive scored for Chelsea against City in a league game at Stamford Bridge. It was already his third goal in four games since the move. The game ended 1-1 but every City fan in the ground had predicted Allen was going to score that day. Once again he had sent a message to Peter Reid.

"I sensed a real opportunity that day. I think even the City fans cheered for me when I scored that day, they certainly never begrudged me that goal. Like I say I'm thankful I still enjoy a relationship with them because it was those fans who made my time up there a special time in my life."

These days Clive is a regular on ITV Sport and has become a well-respected football summariser.

"Funnily enough, Chris Muir, a director up there in my time, was the one who pushed me to go into television, he said I'd be a natural at it. I saw him recently and we had a good laugh about how it's gone. I thoroughly enjoy the TV work."

A shame for him also that the fans didn't pick the team in his time at City as he would have featured more prominently in the starting XI.

CLIVE **WILSON**
26ᵀᴴ DECEMBER 1985
FIRST DIVISION
CITY 1 LIVERPOOL 0
ATT: 35,384

People tend to remember two goals Clive Wilson scored: one against Liverpool and one against Manchester United. They were both important goals, which secured good results against opposition that City struggled against for the majority of the 1980s. It was a dismal era, a see-saw time with the thrills and spills of promotion closely followed by the utter despair of yet another relegation. If there were some good times in the 1980s, well, they didn't last very long.

Clive Wilson was a fine player. One who could and should have become England's first choice left back were it not for the outstanding form of Stuart Pearce and Kenny Sansom. He played most of his City career in left midfield but he showed extra versatility when he moved onto QPR and Tottenham and didn't just do well there but positively excelled as a defender.

Born and bred in Moss Side, Clive moved to Rusholme in the late 60s attending primary school on Heald Place just round the corner from Maine Road. Every other Saturday Clive would see the sights and hear the sounds of the devoted faithful making their way to the match to watch City play.

"I signed for City late on in my developing years. I went to school, Wilbraham High, and then went to college for 2 years. Like Paul Power who was at university I didn't actually sign from apprentice, I was doing electronics at Openshaw Tech but at the same time I started training with City two days a week. Most players that come through the ranks get picked up a lot earlier than I did - at 14, 15 or 16. I honestly thought that chance had passed me by. I don't know, I must have been a late developer or something! I lived in Acomb Street, I suppose you could say it was a long goal kick away from Maine Road. I wasn't really a City fan though. I was a Liverpool fan! Call me a glory hunter, but they were the team back then."

Like a lot of players who end up at full back, Clive was spotted in a much more forward position as a youngster. He takes up the tale. "I was a left winger at youth level and then later left midfield. It was John Bond who switched me to left midfield. He tried me there in a reserve game, I did quite well there and I ended up staying there. I filled in a lot of positions when people were injured. Mr Versatility I think they call it! I was just too young to feature in the Central League team of 1978 that won the league but I just kept on plugging away hoping that my time would come. Malcolm Allison came in and the club was in real turmoil, no doubt about it. Under Mal I'd not been part of the first team squad or anything although I was only a first year apprentice at this time.

"It was John Bond who tried me out at left back and it was mainly here where I played when the first choice was unavailable. It was an important time for me because I was considering my future. Johnny Bond was turning the club around with the FA Cup and League Cup runs and finally gave me my debut in the League Cup in 1981-82 - we beat Wolves 1-0. Up to then I'd been shadowing Asa Hartford and Tommy Booth, learning from them and biding my time."

For Wilson, Maine Road was a home from home. He really enjoyed his time there and couldn't wait to get to work each morning. Or so you'd think...

"Considering I lived literally right around the corner from Maine Road, the amount of times I used to be late for training was unbelievable! Training was every day at 9.45am in the Billy Mac era. I figured I could take this a bit easier than the guys who had to

ABOVE:
Clive was
recognised as
one of the best
young full-
backs in the
country when
he broke into
the City team
in the early
eighties

drive in on the motorway every day, so I treated myself to a nice lie-in and figured if I left the house at 9.40, then it would be five minutes maximum to get there and I'd be on time, but I was late loads of times and no-one could believe it.

"I couldn't blame the motorways or public transport or whatever. I had to start driving to work because it was literally three turns out of my street and if I put my foot down I could get there in just under two minutes from closing my front door! Being a Mancunian playing for Manchester City at that time was absolutely brilliant for me. A wonderful experience in those days. I felt a lot of pride and when I used to go out people would come and talk to you in the street and treat you well.

"People in my local community knew who I was and that I played for City but there was never anything amazing about it in their eyes. I was just a local lad playing for the local team. These days, with footballers being much more high profile, perhaps more of a fuss would have been made about it. Even then, footballers always had better wages than the 9-to-5 workers, but I don't know, you've got to be more dedicated as well these days.

"I had a good rapport with the City fans though. There were a lot of home grown players in the side at that time. The fans could see that, they could see you were trying and I think gave me a little more time to settle in because of this. With other signings, perhaps they're looking for instant results but after I'd found my feet, I'd like to think I showed everybody what I could do."

Yet as Clive found his feet all around him seemed to fall apart. In 1983 John Bond walked out and the club faced a harrowing relegation battle, Clive felt helpless. "Like a lot of our first team squad at that time, I was injured and had I been fit I might have been able to do something about the situation. For Luton 1983 I was sat in the stand when Antic scored that goal and David Pleat ran all over our pitch. I was ready to make my mark in the first team and we were getting relegated.

"I was loaned out to Chester when John Bond was the City manager, while I was there he was replaced by John Benson caretaker until the end of the season. John Benson was replaced by Billy McNeill and I had agreed to sign permanently for Chester for the following season. Billy Mac said he wanted me to stay and try to get into the team."

The early eighties in downtown Manchester was a humdrum time. So The Smiths said anyway. Not exactly the *Ghost Town* The Specials sang about, but still, probably too much fighting on the dance floor. As a young man with a few quid in his pocket and hero-worship guaranteed from the blue half of the city, Wilson used to frequent the city's nightspots and let his hair down.

"I was always into soul music, R&B. Soul music was my first love although I liked a little reggae and jazz too. I was a regular on the Northern Soul circuit I'd be down in Blackpool or at Wigan Pier, we'd certainly end up in places like Rafters and Legends in Manchester - also the club Peter Stringfellow had...was it the Millionaire? I went to some other dingy little places near Victoria Station... but they were good days.

"I'm a Manchester lad and all my friends and family are back there but I've been down here in London now for 15 years so I suppose this place is like home as well these days. When I go back to Manchester it is impressive

> "I was always into soul music, R&B. Soul music was my first love although I liked a little reggae and jazz too. I was a regular on the Northern Soul circuit I'd be down in Blackpool or at Wigan Pier, we'd certainly end up in places like Rafters and Legends in Manchester"

though. They've done up the town centre and people actually live in the city centre, which never used to be the case in my day."

1983 saw The Blues kick off life in the Second Division. One of the early wins came down at Ninian Park. "I remember that game particularly, only because I scored and that in itself was a rarity and we won 3-0 which sort of kick started our season. We were always close to the promotion places but never quite close enough. We lost our form later on and ended up a good 10 points adrift of the three promoted sides.

"The following season I picked up a bad injury, I think it was against Wimbledon's Glyn Hodges in January that year, and it ruled me out for quite a while. The week after we went on a trip to Malaysia! That was fantastic. City didn't have much money at the time but we still went on some amazing trips to America, Australia, Malaysia. Whether it was to promote the name of Manchester City round the world I'm not sure and we didn't see that much of these places because we were training, playing then sleeping so although these were incredible places we didn't see an awful lot.

"Obviously when you're abroad you get to discover different cultures, different ways of life. Mark Lillis, as we all know, is well into his curries. I think the food was pretty nice over there but if it was up to Lillis, we'd have had our bonding holidays on 'Curry Mile' on Wimslow Road!

"I think the food was pretty nice over there [in Malaysia] but if it had been up to Lillis, we'd have had our bonding holidays on curry mile on Wimslow Road!"

"While I was in Malaysia my injury got infected which obviously didn't help my recovery. There was a problem in hospital when they were trying to drain fluid out of my leg or something. It ruled me out for the rest of the season, including the Charlton 5-1 in May which was disappointing."

Promotion saw Wilson back to full

fitness and back in the top flight. The City side was almost a full side of Mancunians, but it didn't help in the first derby of the season. A 0-3 reverse that saw nearly as much action off the pitch as on it meant the return game at Old Trafford was one City dare not lose.

"They were always tough games against United. They had Bryan Robson, Norman Whiteside, Gordon Strachan, Remi Moses... they weren't the softest team in the midfield department were they? But we gave as good as we got. Obviously it was the day before the Full Members' Cup Final and that was a tough weekend of football. We did well to recover in the derby really and at 2-0 down it was all going wrong. One of our goals was down to an Arthur Albiston own goal, whereas mine... well the ball came in from the right hand side and I remember steeping so low, that was the only way I was going to make it. Of course in it went and that was a great feeling. To come from 2-0 down in a derby, especially away from home, you're always going to take that, aren't you?

"I don't want to demean the Full Members' Cup. It was a great occasion to play on the hallowed turf of Wembley and, although it wasn't one of the so-called glamour games, a great occasion all the same. Any player who has played at Wembley, whatever the occasion, will tell you how great an experience it was. We lost 5-4 after coming back from 5-1. Although Chelsea played I think Grimsby the day before this can't be used as an excuse for our defeat as they were the better team on the day. We went 1-0 up and I think we just took our foot off the pedal. We'd put a lot of mental and physical effort into recovering the derby result the day before."

Clive's other magic moment was the winner, a rare one for City at that, against then champions Liverpool at Maine Road on Boxing Day 1985. As Clive was a boyhood Liverpool fan, did it make the goal any more special for him?

"No, not really. Once you sign for a team you let your feelings for other clubs go and I was 100% City when I played there and scored that goal. It didn't mean any more or less than scoring against any other team, but it was a good goal to score against a high-flying side which gave us an important result. We stole that game if we're honest. We were absolutely battered into submission for the whole game. Think of the players they had; Souness, Molby, Whelan all the great players and time after time Liverpool were moving forward on our goal and for whatever reason they couldn't score.

"It got to half time and it was still 0-0 and we hadn't really created a chance. Absolutely nothing. I came off thinking 'wow, we're still in this, but they're going to score pretty shortly.' As the game went on and they still missed loads of chances, we started to feel a little more confident, we were looking round each other saying, 'c'mon, we can win this one!' The ball came in from the left at the Platt Lane end and it looped to the back post towards me. I placed my header down and it went between Grobbelaar's legs. It was the 87th minute and to be honest, we probably still expected to lose, or for Liverpool to come back at us. It was a season of consolidation that one and it was the best result of that season. So it's nice to be remembered for that.

"These days I still get back to Manchester to see family and friends and just recently I saw the last ever game at Maine Road against Southampton and the opener in the new stadium against Barcelona. City are on the up and it's great to see. I'd also like to place on record my thanks to the supporters who backed me during my time at the club."

City fans were sorry to see Clive Wilson go. His contribution in one of City's darkest eras hasn't been forgotten.

DAVID **WHITE**
24TH APRIL 1991
FIRST DIVISION
ASTON VILLA 1 CITY 5
ATT: 24,168

It's the day after the Soccer Sixes at the MEN Arena where David White has just led City to a resounding win in the regional heats of the now traditional close-season veterans tournament. City were beaten by Liverpool - nothing new there then - but overall the night was a success and this morning Whitey's ankle is playing up again, a reminder of the injuries which stopped a fine career in its tracks.

"Last year I was ineligible to play but I'm 35 now and that means I'm qualified," he says. David White, a veteran? Is this the same David White who I watched and idolised when I was a kid growing up on the Kippax? The same David White who scored a hat-trick in the 10-1, who played a starring role in the 5-1, the David White who played in the famous five alongside Lake, Redmond, Brightwell and Hinchcliffe?

"Perhaps I could've played to a later age," he muses "but at Leeds I had 2 serious operations and then I broke my heel so it didn't help... but it was fantastic to pull on that blue shirt one more time last night."

I ask him if the surface of the Arena was like the famous plastic pitch at Oldham, scene of his hat-trick in that end of season 5-2 goal bonanza. On the contrary, it was more like the Pitz at Ardwick, "It was a very thin roll of carpet over a flat concrete surface. So the ball ran true and quick but when you are running about it doesn't give your ankle much in the way of support. Liverpool attacked us more than they attacked anyone else, but you know, we were just conserving ourselves for the final!"

If you consider that Whitey started training with

City's junior teams back in 1978 and he is still technically turning out for them now, then it can be argued that David White has really devoted his whole life to the City cause.

"I was playing as a ten-year-old for Eccles Boys Under-11 team and we were thrashed 4-0 by a team called Whitehill, but I must've had a good game because the City scout invited me for a trial. So I was playing for City's nursery teams and I even trained with Trevor Francis when he was at the club! When I was with Eccles Boys I was a Manchester City season ticket holder and from that time on, every school holiday we'd have I'd be back down at City training and playing at places like Platt Lane."

White signed professional forms in October 1985 and went onto make his league debut at Luton Town in September 1986 but it wasn't until much later that he got a real run in the first team. His career up until then had been under the stewardship of youth team manager Tony Book or 'Skip' as he was universally known. Whilst it's well known what Tony Book achieved as a player and as first team manager, less recognised are his feats of bringing on City's youth team of the mid 1980s culminating in the 1986 FA Youth Cup triumph over Manchester United.

"I had a decent first year at City, I played in the A team and the youth team and I even featured in some reserve games whilst I was still at school. By this time I'd begun to realise that we had on our hands an exceptional crop of youngsters at the club. We lost one game, 4-0 at South Liverpool I think, but from then on, we didn't even draw a game. We used to thrash United 'A', Liverpool 'A' and Everton 'A', all our major rivals and to be honest we could've won the Youth Cup the year before but we went out up at Newcastle on an icy pitch in 1985.

"We were first year apprentices and the second year apprentices included the likes of Darren Beckford,

John Beresford and Earl Barrett. In the second cup run we came to the fore and throughout that season we were taking opposing teams apart. Forest, we beat them 8-0, another team from the Middlesbrough area called Billingham, who fancied themselves a bit, we went up there and beat them 10-0, we had some truly remarkable victories."

One point made by City fans over the years concerns the number of great players the club have produced who should not have been allowed to leave. For the first time certainly that I can remember, David White offers an insight as to what the selection process was like in those days, "Booky was a very strict disciplinarian. Those who toed his line went onto succeed at City. Those who didn't moved on. We were doing very well but Booky couldn't afford us to start getting complacent, he wouldn't allow it. John Beresford, Earl Barrett and Darren Beckford didn't push on at City but as you've seen had good careers elsewhere. Ashley Ward, Neil Lennon, Gerry Taggart, Michael Hughes, Shez [Mike Sheron] all had a brilliant schooling at City and although they didn't stay with City, they still managed to play on in the game successfully.

"Forest are renowned for having great kids and at the time they had another fine crop, including Franz Carr, their winger. We dicked them 8-0 and we're coming off the field and all Booky would say is 'Well done, good performance lads, now get out there and replace the divots.' So we're all out on the pitch at 10 o'clock at night, having just murdered Forest, doing these menial tasks. I'm not sure if the academy staff are allowed to treat the youngsters in the same way but it never did us any harm, it kept our feet on the ground and stopped us getting too big-headed. He had to be like that, he knew what he was doing to keep us progressing.

"Glyn Pardoe was there and he'd be the one who'd

put his arm round you and pick you back up - but it was the right combination. We'd win 3- or 4-nil and in the dressing room Booky would be lamenting the passing or saying we should have had seven or eight. That's how we kept improving. We couldn't afford to stand still. It was healthy though, you'd have some praise but then they'd keep on at you at your bad points. If you turned up one day and Skip didn't like your hair then he'd tell you so!

"In the summertime we'd be there from 9am to 3.30pm cleaning out the baths or cleaning out the toilets, polishing boots and tidying things up. We all thought at the time, 'God, this is a long day', but when you look back at it, it wasn't really at all. It fostered good team spirit, it made us so together that it used to show out there on the pitch. Someone like Stevie Redmond, I mean, these days we see a lot less of each other but we met up recently and it was like seeing your best friend from school.

"There was a time for about two years where we were in each others' pockets all the time - we even went away on holiday a few times. There's other lads who were fine players that came through at that time. Paul Moulden of course scored goals for fun and continued that even in the lower leagues. Andy Thackeray, he's played at Wrexham, Rochdale, Nuneaton Borough - he's had a full career in the game.

"In the semi in '86 we met Arsenal who I think had Michael Thomas and Merse playing amongst others - that was a tough tie but we came through and then of course, the final was a Manchester derby, a 2-0 win at home and a 1-1 draw away. There was a brilliant turn out from the City fans, officially it was 18,000 but they opened up other stands and I'm sure a lot more were present, whichever way you look at it, there was a bigger crowd than there was at Old Trafford."

So, a tough background and some hard graft had moulded the already talented White into a winner.

He was ready for the first team, ready to take on all before him and he had no fear.

"In hindsight, City getting relegated did our generation a slight favour in that the club could throw us all in together, in a slightly easier league. Had we stayed up we didn't quite have the finances in place to buy the old heads needed to give us that combination required to survive in the top flight. The infrastructure was not quite right at the club - I mean Lakey and Bobby [Brightwell] had been given a few games but 1987-88 was the first real year we all played together and we had some superb results that season."

Certainly, it would have been a proud moment for Tony Book and Glyn Pardoe as they watched the lads they nurtured winning England Under-21 honours. In addition to White, Steve Redmond, captain of that triumphant FA Youth Cup side, was voted Supporters' Player of the Year in his first full season and became the youngest player to captain the first team. Then there was Paul Lake, who had been close to a place in the 1990 England World Cup squad - in fact Bobby Robson told him it was only his lack of experience at the top level that prevented his selection. Lakey was tipped to be a future England captain before injury intervened. Andy Hinchcliffe went on to win full England honours and Ian Brightwell became a real fans' favourite. All of these City-reared youngsters went on to represent England at one level or another. Yet as far as White is concerned, they were just the tip of the iceberg.

"We also had Paul Moulden, Paul Simpson on the left, Jason Beckford, Paul Stewart and Tony Adcock up

"In the summertime we'd be there from 9am to 3.30pm cleaning out the baths or cleaning out the toilets, polishing boots and tidying things up. We all thought at the time 'God, this is a long day' but when you look back... it fostered good team spirit, it made us so together that it used to show out there on the pitch."

front - so in those days I never got a game as a striker because my role was to provide service to the likes of Paul Stewart. Mel made me defend slightly more than I wanted to but he wanted wide players to help keep the shape of the team by defending as well as attacking. Training with him was brilliant though. Every day was a little bit different.

"I had a spell at Leeds where the training was abysmal. After first team training I used to spend an hour training with the kids and Paul Hart because it was so much more interesting. Whether you're in the first team or not you need that training routine to be of use to you. Under Mel it was terrific. Mel had some back problems and so John Deehan took over the training routines. Maybe it wasn't as good as under Mel but it still helped us gain promotion in the spring of 1989."

Season 1987-88 was a goal bonanza for City with the Blues breaking their two-year awayday hoodoo with a 4-2 thumping of then league leaders Bradford City at Valley Parade, having been 2-0 down. The legendary 10-1 win over Huddersfield Town was followed up by a midweek 6-2 Simod Cup win over Plymouth Argyle - Tony Adcock scoring two hat-tricks in a week. There was a further six-goal drubbing for the Pilgrims in the League Cup down at Home Park and a 3-0 win over Nottingham Forest in the League Cup in the days when Forest were undoubtedly one of the best and most consistent teams in the country.

City being City though, the Blues still managed to lose 1-0 in the return game against Huddersfield even though the Yorkshire side were odds-on certainties for the drop! Whitey rose to prominence during some of these games, scooping the Barclays 'Young Eagle of the Month' award for November 1987 after scoring seven goals in five games. Liverpool, in those days the all-conquering red machine, were supposedly interested in some of the City starlets. In the 1988 FA Cup quarter-final City and Liverpool drew 44,000 to Maine Road and, though the watching millions would have sat up and taken notice of the Boy Blues, in the end it was still men against boys and a 4-0 home defeat. Nevertheless, it gave young White a taste of things to come.

OPPOSITE: White's pace lent another dimension to City's attack under Reid. His partnership with Niall Quinn helping City to a top five finish.

With promotion achieved in heart-stopping fashion on the final day of the following season, City turned their attentions to the top flight. The 5-1 humiliation of Manchester United is well documented elsewhere in this book and although White didn't score that day, his cross for David Oldfield opened the floodgates on an afternoon of pride for Manchester City. Things soon went wrong though and by December City had slipped to the bottom of the league.

"I was a fan of Mel Machin's training but first and foremost I was a fan of Manchester City and we were destroyed 6-0 at Derby and things were falling apart again. So for that reason I wasn't sad to see Mel go. Mel's done well in his career since, he's a great bloke and I have great respect for him but when we moved to bring Howard Kendall in, I was delighted by the appointment."

The history books show that Kendall's era was highly

successful. He dragged the club off the bottom of the table and left the club in a healthy fifth place. Under Kendall, White also developed further, increasing his goal tally and goal assist ratio too.

"When we signed Niall Quinn he called me and Mark Ward in for a chat and said, 'we've got a proper centre-forward now and I want us to give him the service he needs. I want one of you to play on the left and one of you on the right'. Wardy immediately put his hand up and volunteered the left wing which was great for me because I didn't really want to play there. Well, I thought this was fantastic management from Kendall to get the players involved like that.

"He explained that he felt he had a back four that was solid enough to cope with anything thrown at them and we were solid in midfield with Reidy and now we had a target man to aim for too. What people don't realise is that Howard rebuilt the spine of the club. Alan Harper was always going to play, whether it was at left back or at sweeper. Kendall said when he arrived that we weren't going to go out and win games, we were to try and not lose them first of all. In the midfield Reidy was his general and upfront Inchy [Adrian Heath] would play mostly off Quinny with Clive Allen only playing now and again.

"All of us in the dressing room were aware of the feelings of the fans towards some of his decisions but as a squad we were 100% behind Howard because he knew what he was doing. We knew the fans had their favourites like Ian Bishop and Clive Allen but Kendall had filled the spine of his team with players who'd won the League, the FA Cup and the European Cup Winners' Cup.

"I always felt that some of his decisions received a lukewarm reception and I believe that if he'd have had a warmer welcome at the start, then he may not have been so inclined to return to Everton."

"The fans' argument was that Inchy only scored one goal all season whereas Clive Allen was on the bench. However, much as we respected Clive and loved him, none of us believed he should've replaced Inchy in the starting XI. What I found disappointing was that the fans ignored all the good work Inchy did for the team.

"During the times when he was playing, I scored about 17 goals, Mark Ward notched about 14, Quinny 20 odd, Clive Allen 9 or 10 coming off the bench. We were scoring goals as a team so frankly it's irrelevant that our second striker wasn't scoring regularly. Our two wingers chipped in with 35 goals. Who's to say that if Clive Allen replaced Inchy the rest of the team's goals wouldn't have dried up.

"Kendall said on leaving that City was his love affair and Everton was his marriage and it must've been a tremendous emotional pull to return to Goodison Park. But I always felt that some of his decisions received a lukewarm reception and I believe that if he'd have had a warmer welcome at the start, then he may not have been so inclined to return to Everton."

The fans saw one of their heroes, Andy Hinchcliffe, replaced by Neil 'dissa' Pointon, another Goodison old boy. Keeper Andy Dibble made way for new £1m man Tony Coton, who had some baggage from his time at Birmingham and Watford. On top of all that, fans' darling Ian Bishop was sacrificed along with Trevor Morley in a deal that brought Mark Ward from West Ham. Whether the fans simply resented their Merseyside connections or feared that City were turning into Everton reserves, the fact remains that after that initial scepticism, the fans took Coton, Pointon and Ward to their hearts. Under Kendall both City's and White's fortunes took a shot in the arm and as White himself says, "I believe we could have won the league before United, had Kendall stayed. I certainly believe we would have won trophies in his time at the very least."

Kendall would have been regarded as a hero had City held onto a 3-1 lead in the 1990 Maine Road derby, a game in which White was denied a hat-trick by the crossbar, having scored a a spectacular second following an exquisite flick from the heel of Adrian Heath. Heath was cast as villain for missing a sitter in the November '91 derby, only for him to make amends three days later with two goals down at QPR in the League Cup, a performance that prompted the City fans to chorus, 'and now you're gonna believe us, Adrian Heath is back!'

"Back when Kendall resigned," continues White, "the players had gone to Peter Swales and actually asked if the club would instate Peter Reid as player-manager. He had the respect of everyone and we knew everything was right behind the scenes and we could carry on as normal. I'm glad to say Peter Swales took this on board."

Whereas under Kendall, White had predominantly stayed on the wing, providing the ammo with deep crosses for Quinn, he started to drift further forward under Reid until he'd been converted into a striker.

Kendall had gone but City and in particular White were producing some devastating form. Niall Quinn scored his one and only hat-trick for City down at Selhurst Park as City trounced Steve Coppell's third-placed Eagles 3-1. The following week, the fans at Maine Road enjoyed an easy win over a skilful Forest side, with three goals wrapping the game up within the first half hour. Onto fourth-placed Leeds, who would win the championship the following year, and a brilliant 2-1 win for City - Andy Hill and Quinn on target for the Blues. Down at Highbury White's pace unhinged the famous Arsenal defence and City held the Gunners after being 2-0 down.

Back at Maine Road, Niall Quinn scored his 20th goal of the season, then went in net and saved Dean Saunders' penalty as City beat Derby County 2-1, relegating Arthur Cox's Rams in the process. Even with ten men, City kept on attacking and David White made the game safe with a blistering left-foot drive from 20 yards. City also relegated Sunderland by beating them 3-2 in front of 40,000 on a sun-baked final afternoon of the season at Maine Road. White's last-minute winner ensured that City finished above United for the first time in over a decade.

The only blip in this sequence was the 1-0 defeat at Old Trafford, where Colin Hendry's unfortunate own goal gave the hosts an unlikely 1-0 win in the run-up to the 1991 European Cup Winners' Cup Final in Rotterdam. This game was the second consecutive derby at Old Trafford where the home team hadn't sold all their tickets. On this day Barcelona scarves were spotted in the Stretford Paddock as hundreds of Blues took advantage of the £15 pay at the gate fee. On the pitch, City's plans for the derby had been thrown into disarray when they lost Tony Coton to suspension for a glove-throwing incident in the Derby game which meant 19-year-old novice Martyn Margetson made his debut in front of 46,000 people.

In the middle of this sequence one result shines out and remains David White's most memorable game for Manchester City. It was the night City looked like Real Madrid in their all white kit... and gave a performance which was all White on the night!

"Villa Park was my favourite away ground and it was balmy that night, when I notched up 50 league goals for Manchester City. We got off to a dream start inside the first five minutes, a long punt forward by Coton was flicked on by Quinny and I struck it sweetly left footed across Nigel Spink into the far corner. The second followed soon after. Again it was Quinny who set me up and I raced through to lob Spink for 2-0. I think Andy Comyn was marking me that night with Paul McGrath much further forward than usual, they deployed him as a central midfielder. At 2-0 they were chasing the game so they put him back to defence and changed the formation a bit and to be honest they had us under the cosh for the rest of the first half.

"Quinny made so many goals for me it was untrue. I used to stand level with the centre-half and I used to mark the centre-half, in other words the opposite of the norm. I knew Quinny would get to the ball first and so my job was to get to the ball first, wherever it landed. The ball could go anywhere but I had to be ready for it and 9 times out of 10 I'd get there first, if it was a straight race between me and the centre half. If the centre-half was quick, we'd put Shez [Mike Sheron] through the middle and I'd drift wide, especially if I was playing someone like Stuart Pearce because I knew I could beat him for pace. Against someone else though, I'd play through the middle and this is what happened at Villa Park."

5-1 is something of a favourite scoreline amongst Manchester City fans. We had it against Schalke, against Charlton, against United and much later

also against Barnsley when the First Division title was secured but on this occasion no one had gone along expecting another five-goal blast. Half time came and White, by now eager to notch his 50th goal for The Blues, knew it was on and was busting a gut to do it.

"We were hitting them on the break and I managed to get away down the right. I put a ball across the box to Mark Brennan, who side-footed it home for 3-0."

Villa were then awarded a penalty when Colin Hendry was adjudged to have handled in the box. The City players crowded the referee, incensed with the decision, the game might have been in the bag already but it was quite apparent how much City wanted to win every decision. David Platt converted the resulting penalty - his second against the Blues that season.

Opposite: David White slots the second of four goals he scored in his favourite game at Villa Park.

The finish for White's hat-trick goal was straight out of the top drawer and it was a special moment for him, "As a kid, I'd dreamt of a moment like this. I'd also practised for ages and ages at bending a ball round the keeper at pace so when Quinny slid in and won me the ball, it sat up nicely for me to do this. I tried it, it came off and for me it was just a dream goal."

White rubbed more salt into Villa's wounds with a fifth that went in off the post from the edge of the box after cutting inside from the left. The Villa game put White firmly in the spotlight and at this time the press were simply raving about him. The clamour for a full England call-up gathered momentum and the following season saw further highlights.

A Geoff Hurst type goal (landing on the line having hit the bar) saw off Liverpool during a blistering start to the campaign that saw City go top of the league. Two more peaches against Grobbelaar in the return at Anfield, one a lob from the touchline, gave players and fans real delight. His cracker of a Christmas continued with the winner against champions Arsenal and White's goals in the new year kept City well in the title race until late on. Again City finished fifth but a hat-trick on the final day at Oldham gave White 21 goals for the season.

Then, following seven goals in seven games at the start of 1992-93, the England call up finally came for White for the game in Santander against Spain, a game all City fans seem to remember.

"I am eternally grateful to Graham Taylor that he gave me an England cap but perhaps my confidence suffered as a result of the way he treated me afterwards. I think 20 players were called up for that game, which at the time, were the best 20 players England had available. John Barnes and Trevor Steven, players who would've featured, were injured and Rod Wallace, who may have got the nod before me, also picked up a knock the Sunday before. So to get in the starting XI and to make myself a couple of good opportunities at international level was fantastic. I could have scored, on another day they'd have gone in but I would've appreciated maybe a phone call from Taylor when the next squad was announced just to explain why I was the one making way again.

"I was immensely disappointed that I didn't get into the following England squads, but then again if Barnesy or Trevor Steven had been dropped for me, they'd have been disappointed too."

"To me, Peter Reid did a great job for City. Alright the money he spent in bringing Curley and Phelo in raised questions but for whatever reason he stopped getting money and that's where it started to go wrong."

As David's confidence took a knock, so City's form became more inconsistent. The make or break 1993 FA Cup quarter-final against Tottenham became something of a watershed for the club. The 4-2 defeat and subsequent pitch invasion left the Blues treading water for years to come.

"To me," argues White, "Peter Reid did a great job for City. Alright, the money he spent in bringing Curley and Phelo in raised questions but for whatever reason he stopped getting money and that's where it started to go wrong. The way he was treated over the John Maddock thing was embarrassing really but if you look back at that time, we finished ninth and before that fifth twice, which would almost be a Champions League place now. We would've been in Europe then had it not been for the European ban."

David White achieved a huge amount during his time at Manchester City. His story is a fascinating insight into what went right and wrong in the late 80s and early 90s at City. One thing is for sure, he gave the fans some brilliant memories. Anyone who was at Villa Park on that night in May '91 can vouch for that. A Blue through and through and to some of us, twentysomethings who used to stand on the Kippax and can just about recall his early days in the relegation season in 1986-87 - he remains one of our favourite players.

IAN BISHOP
17ᵀᴴ DECEMBER 1989
FIRST DIVISION
EVERTON 0 CITY 0
ATT: 21,737

Ian Bishop is a Blue. Always has been from the moment he signed for City. Always will be till the day he dies. I'm in his pub in Birkdale near Southport, a beautiful part of the world. It's a footy pub. Ian charms his regulars with tales of his Maine Road days. A dad and his five-year-old son come to the bar. The little lad is wearing a United shirt. "Sorry you're barred, this is a City pub," laughs Bishop. The lad looks bemused. "Did he play for Man City, dad?" "Yes son, he did," replies the dad. Five minutes later the lad returns. "My dad said you were a dead good footballer, can you come outside and play with us for 10 minutes?" "No problem," says Bishop, who drops everything and has a kick around outside.

"You've got to show them the way," he says later, "even if he is a red. It's not his fault, it's just because they're a fashionable team, it's peer pressure. He'll probably be a blue though in two or three years."

Bishop's pub attracts the local football glitterati - Hansen, Lawrenson, Mark Wright, Howard Kendall. Steve McMahon and wife are over at the bar right now. Scousers everywhere! Bishop is a blue now, but in the football mad city of Liverpool was he a Toffee or a Kop-ite?

"I was an Arsenal fan as a kid. Charlie George, '71 Cup final. I must have been the only Arsenal fan in Liverpool. I went to Anfield a lot as a kid as Everton were awful - you wouldn't have gone to Goodison in those days - I used to watch good football! People ask me why I, a Scouser, was supporting Arsenal? But I used to say to people Charlie George, Liam Brady...

what two better players could you have to look up to.

"My boy was six when he latched onto Robbie Fowler. So he became a Liverpool fan. Then he went to Leeds so he became a Leeds fan. Now he's at City so he's actually a Man City fan so it's worked out alright in the end. But you stick with people at an early age and what Charlie George did, lying down on the Wembley turf after scoring, always stuck with me.

"It's fortunate the way things work out, after Charlie it was Liam Brady, he was my next hero. Luckily enough, I played alongside Brady in his last nine games for West Ham, so if you're asking me about the highlights of my career, well, you've got to include that, you know, playing with your heroes."

Ian Bishop spent the majority of his career at City and West Ham, but he also had spells at Carlisle and Bournemouth. He even went over to the States for a while too, but more of that later. He started his career at Everton and as every Blue knows, 1989 was the second time that Kendall had got rid of Bishop. The first time was back in his Everton days so they must have been painful times, but did Bishop accept Kendall's reasons?

"I don't want to disappoint anybody but he's a decent fella, he's a lovely fella, he comes in here in fact. He was right the first time round, probably right the second time round too - it just didn't make me or the fans happy. I just don't understand why he didn't latch onto me. I was 19 and his reason was that I hadn't progressed as quickly as he thought I would have done, but at the same time I had 12 midfield players in my way, so going from the 'A' team I couldn't have progressed anyway.

"There was Trevor [Steven], Sheeds [Kevin Sheedy], Reidy, Bracewell, Kevin Richardson, Trevor Ross, Andy King, Alan Ainscough, John McMahon - Stevie's older brother, Alan Harper even played in midfield and that's not all of them. When he arrived he bought about 16 players - I was about 16 or 17 at the time and they were all still there by the time I was 19, so I was playing 'A' team football when I should've been playing reserve team football. So I could understand why he said I didn't progress but at the same time he was hindering my path!"

Kendall didn't seem the sort to tolerate any misbehaviour, were there any drinking incidents that forced the issue here at all?

"No because I didn't start drinking until I left, so it wasn't anything to do with that. Players do drink. Premier League players don't do it as much now because there's too much at stake with the press and everything else but I had run-ins with Harry Redknapp all my life. You're not allowed to drink 48 hours before a game, right, so on a Wednesday night, which was your last possible night to have a drink, which was a better night than a Monday or Tuesday when you'd go somehere like the Conti in Liverpool. Then, on a Wednesday night, I'm going out on the beer. I'm a footballer fair enough, but before that, I'm a man and I need to do what I feel like doing.

"Come the Thursday morning, I'd turn up on time, train properly with everyone else and Harry would still turn around and say, 'You're stinking of beer!' and I'd say 'Yeah, that's because last night, I went out and I had a load of beer!' I said, 'Listen, if I ever let you down on a Saturday, take the shirt off me!' and he never did... for eight or nine years at least. I'm assistant now at Burscough Town to Mike Marsh and I get to play too, but I could never be a full-time

manager. You turn turkey! It's like you're moving over to the dark side!

"So I left Everton and moved to Carlisle United. I went there for four years but people don't realise they were in the old Second Division in those days. I scored at Maine Road in 1984. In my first season we won 3-1, when there was only a couple of games left that season. It was on Match of the Day and we were in that red kit. David Phillips opened the scoring with a real beauty but then we just took over. I scored from a header, flicked on from a corner, Platt Lane End. I watched it that night on the telly!

"So I've played up at Carlisle and then down south at Bournemouth which means I can settle anywhere, you can't go much further north or south than those two. It's always been about playing football for me. I gave up a lot of money when I left West Ham to return to City, don't get me wrong, I got a great deal off City but at the time people talking to me were saying 'it's ludicrous what you're doing, going to a Second Division club.' Alright, they were still in the First Division at the time but they were more or less on their way down. There was a chance we could stay up but I've got to be honest I didn't contribute too much that year. I wasn't match fit. I'd been on the bench 23 times and only got on three times so obviously when I moved, it takes you five or six matches to settle in but that was all that was left. Wherever you go, you need that length of time, to get to know people properly. Joe ended up leaving me out at the end of that season and he was probably right to do so."

As Bishop himself says, he made a long move south from Brunton Park to Dean Court, which meant more games against Manchester City in 1988-89. On May 8th 1989 the Cherries were the visitors to Maine Road. Two goals from Paul Moulden and one from Trevor Morley gave The Blues an unassailable 3-0 lead at half time... or so everyone thought...

"One game that will always stick with me, one of the games I enjoyed the most, was the 3-3 at City when I played for Bournemouth. I'd heard a few whispers beforehand there were a few rumours about City's interest previously. Kenny Dalglish was in the stand that day watching me. There was talk of England and all this, that I was the next Bryan Robson! I mean, I wasn't fit to lace Robson's boots on or off the pitch. Tried me best off the field though! My agent Jerome Anderson, I say my agent, I got sort of introduced to him about three games before the end of that season, was one of Harry's mates, so I felt a move was on the cards.

"But I'd heard the City rumours that they wanted me and it was the day they'd have gone up and had the lads clinched promotion that afternoon they would have all been off to Australia that night and they were going to play the reserves at Bradford. This is what I got told after I finally signed for City and became friends with all the players - so, as you can imagine, being part of the side that fought back from 3-0 down, they all had a bit of a pop at me! People say was it Mel's tactics that day but I think it was just the way the game panned out. I actually thought we [Bournemouth] were the better side at 3-0 down, we'd had a lot of the ball and it was an open game which is how the game should be played in my book. The seven minutes' injury time gave us time to claw it back - but if you're a City fan, you can't complain though - look what happened at Wembley in the play-off final!

"We were a good team that year. I think we finished seventh, just one place off the play-offs and certainly at home we were a tough nut to crack. Nobody came and turned us over at Dean Court. Chelsea, Leeds, Sheffield Wednesday, City - they all had tough, tough games. Jamie Redknapp was there but he was only a baby at the time."

A £750,000 fee secured the services of Bishop that summer and Bishop returned to the north-west. He was finally a City player. Amongst those early highlights was the 5-1 game, which was to endear him to the Manchester City support forever.

"In the first five minutes of that game I think we could have been 3-0 down. If it wasn't for the crowd spilling over and us going off it might have been a different story. I don't think Mel expected a result. At 24, I was one of the oldest players there that day. We had five England Under-21 players and they all seemed to have been groomed just for that day. We were in the bottom three for most of that season but apart from at Derby we never really got turned over by anyone. The defeats were usually by the odd goal and we played good football. I felt a bit sorry for Mel - he was close to delivering a great side and he was a really nice fella and a great coach. He'd tell it how it is, he'd say, 'I'm gonna be honest with you. You may not like what I'm going to tell you, but I'm being honest' and managers sometimes aren't always honest, like when they drop you and cite a squad rotation system. No, it's not squad rotation you're just dropping me, so tell me that!

"As for my goal, the third goal, looking back I didn't know what I was doing there. When Reddo played the ball I was standing about five yards away from him - just outside our penalty box. I thought Dave [Oldfield] isn't getting there, he won't reach Reddo's pass but I've got to go anyway and I remember seeing Incey and I think Incey felt the same thing. So he let me go away from him as he probably thought Oldfield's not going to get there either but he just nicked it in front of Pallister and once that happened I've gone full sprint (which is half pace for everyone else) into their penalty box because I know something's on now.

"I remember thinking I've just got to keep going because if it comes anywhere near me I've got to get on the end of it. It curled towards me and I remember Trevor coming up behind me, so I went for it, falling down but I got a full head on it but I couldn't see where it went. I never saw it go in. I was sliding along the floor with my head upside down thinking the keeper's gonna clatter me. I got up, saw it was in the net and then I just felt so great! Just to play in a game like that, the Manchester derby, is something very special indeed.

"At half time, we calmed down a bit and we had a team talk and when they made it 3-1 I really did think, 'here we go!'. Then Lakey made a run and put Dave in for a tap-in which took the pressure off us but then the fifth goal was the best. What a brilliant run from Hinchy and I take great pleasure in saying this as I always have done, Paul Cooper could have been on the end of it at that stage, we could have pushed him up front, we were battering them so much. I didn't get a pint till half nine that night! I should have stayed in Manchester that night but I went back to Liverpool to see my family but it was chaos with about ten people in the house all trying to get ready! I ended up in the social club or British Legion that night with my old fella - watching the highlights on the screen on Granada!"

Amazing then to think that the 5-1 wasn't Bishop's most memorable game at City. Of course it was one of them, but as Machin made way for Kendall, it meant that Bishop's love affair with the City fans was to be cut short. Before he left though, he was to have a final memorable moment. "The first day of training

OPPOSITE: Bishop was remembered for his stunning performance in the 5-1 - here he celebrates before a euphoric Maine Road

Ian BISHOP

[after Kendall's appointment] was the Friday before the Everton game, the game I've waited for all my life. It had been over five years since I'd last set foot in Goodison Park and here I was sat on the bench, dropped because I didn't figure in his plans. All the City fans are packed like sardines into The Park End screaming 'We want Bishop, we want Bishop!' The whole game I was just sat there and all the City fans were singing my name throughout. Howard wouldn't, couldn't even look at me all day. When he came back from Spain - and ask Lakey about this he'll tell you, - I turned round and said to everyone, 'It's been nice knowing youse.' He went 'Y'what?' and I said, 'I'm off lads.' I knew the writing was on the wall.

"I only scored three goals for City first time round and two of those were headers. United and Luton the following week and the other was a volley against Norwich in the League Cup. I remember coming off the pitch on Boxing Day having played Norwich and I saw all the banners around the stadium, 'Don't Go' and 'Bish please stay!', I was the last off the pitch and I walked off crying my eyes out. They talk about Gazza but I had tears pouring down my face. Howard waited for me at the touchline and hugged me. I really thought it was going to turn around. The next day I went to see him and said 'Has anything changed' and he just said 'No.' I think Howard actually wrote in his autobiography that he never realised just how popular I was here, but it's been and gone now. Inwardly, I'm not as angry now as the fans were - or perhaps still are."

Mark Ward joined City in a move that saw Bishop and City's hero at Valley Parade, Trevor Morley, move south. Bishop was to stay in the East End for

> **"The first day of training [after Kendall's appointment] was the Friday before the Everton game, the game I've waited for all my life. It had been over 5 years since I'd last set foot in Goodison Park and here I was sat on the bench, dropped because I didn't figure in his plans."**

nine years. Most of that time was happy but by the time City came back in for Bishop he had been ready to leave for a long, long time.

"I was out when Joe phoned my house. It was March and I think I'd been offered a one-year deal at West Ham which would've taken me up to my testimonial and I'd sorted all that out with Harry but to be honest, I wasn't happy there anymore, me and him didn't see eye to eye. I felt he was treating me badly and wrongly after all I'd done for him.

"I played for six months with a double hernia because he asked me to and I don't know if you've ever had that but you can't even put your socks on. You can't lift your leg to put your kecks on, you can't sit up to get out of bed. I'd be playing the game on a Saturday, rolling sideaways out of bed on the Sunday so I could actually get up, not train until Friday, jogging on the Friday, just to get the body moving again and then playing again on the Saturday. All because he asked me to and I did that for long six months, they wouldn't treat horses like that.

"For six months I did that because I loved playing football - it was nothing to do with him. Okay, he did ask me, but it wasn't a personal favour. I did it because I loved playing football. I had a cartilage operation at West Ham and I had my first game eight days later. Looking back I snapped two ribs in a game at Luton. Mark Pembridge came across me and elbowed me and they'd snapped completely. It was excruciating pain, I'm lying on the touchline, I'm trying to get my breath and the fans are caning me to get up and on with the game. All the subs are already on so I stayed on for the last half an hour because that's the way I am.

"The very first problem I had at West Ham was when I'd damaged my ankle ligaments in the first half of the last game of the season against Cambridge United, a game we needed to win to clinch promotion.

In the end we did win, 5-0, but I asked the physio at half time to strap it up so I couldn't feel anything below the knee. I wanted to be part of what was happening. I'd waited all season for this and I wasn't going to miss it.

"While the lads are on the champagne I'm not even on any of the photos because I'm in the physio room with a blown-up ankle. I've missed out on all the jollies and all the champers just because I wanted to take my place and play my part in the arena where it really counted - the pitch.

"When I left West Ham I could have sat out the rest of my career on the bench for another season and made a fortune but I didn't want that, I wanted to play football. Managers have it easy, as I said before, they can leave players out and tell them they're 'resting them'. Players accept that and I can't have that. You *must* want to play, it's like when foreigners turn around and say 'we're tired'! If you're tired, take two days off training, don't miss games. Now even at Burscough we had two games in two days in pre-season which is a fitness thing. Now every Easter you play Saturday then Monday and at Christmas I'd play four games in one week - 90 minutes each time. At the highest possible level. Now for the 20-year-old lads at Burscough to say, 'I'm tired - I can't play two games in two days' - *it's ridiculous! Go back to being a little boy!*"

Joe Royle had come in after turning down 14 other managerial jobs to accept the post of City manager, replacing Frank Clark. There was soon to be a new chairman too, but short-term the target was to try and avoid relegation to the third tier of English football. Not even Royle could save the Blues from such a fate - a fate that had been predicted as far back as 1996 by Lincoln boss John Beck who had said, 'Relegation may need to happen again in order that City sort themselves out.' This comment, coming in the wake of an horrific 4-1 League Cup humiliation at Sincil Bank, had angered the board of the time but it appeared that Beck's comments were spot on by the time Bishop re-signed. Bishop had last been at the club after they had trounced United 5-1. Now the trap door to Division Two was opening what were the differences between the two periods and did he ever feel he had made a mistake?

"Do you know the film, *Midnight Express*? We're talking about the difference between the first time round and the second time round, have you seen that film? When they are all in jail in Turkey and they're all walking round in one big circle, no one smiling, all the heads are down. There were 54 pros there and they were all like that, walking round with their heads well down. I hadn't felt it was the wrong move because I understood relegation could happen. It was my club though, City and I came back together because I had some unfinished business from 1989. I'd decided that whatever happens, I'm just going to go to City and play my best for that club. I said at the time money never came into it and it was true."

A 5-2 win at Stoke became irrelevant, City were down with the dead men and the clear out began. Bishop was still there of course, but it wasn't until Stoke were beaten again at Christmas time that a promotion challenge seemed in the offing - even if it was to be via the play-offs.

"I was a sub for the play-off final but I'd pulled my hamstring against York on the last day of the season after just 20 minutes and off I went. The specialist said it was a six-weeker and I said, 'It can't be! We've got Wigan in the semis over two legs. Okay, I'll resign myself to missing that - but six weeks?'

"Do you know the film, *Midnight Express*? When they are all in jail in Turkey and they're all walking round in one big circle, no one smiling, all the heads are down. There were 54 pros there {when I returned to City] and they were all like that, walking round with their heads well down."

"I watched the away leg on the big screen at Maine Road and I had a few beers in the box and then I watched the second leg from the stand at Maine Road where the winner came off one of Shaun's ample breasts! I saw all the City fans going beserk on the pitch and I thought 'there's no way I'm missing Wembley!'

"I said to Joe 'I want to play' and he just said, 'No, you can't play,' but I trained for the whole of that week, I limped through it but I got through it and I didn't want him to see that I wasn't fit. After that week I said, 'Look, you've got to play me.' He said, 'Are you 100% fit?' and I said, 'In my mind I'm 100% fit.' He said, 'I can't do it, what if I start you and then after two minutes you collapse. I've wasted a man, it may go to extra time, I'll have wasted a man.' I said, 'Joe, I'll be fine', so he put me on the bench.

"He [Joe Royle] grabbed me after the match and said 'You changed the game!' I said 'I know I changed the game, it was 0-0 when I came on, it was 2-0 for Gillingham soon afterwards!' He said, 'No - you did change the game, if you hadn't been on there things wouldn't have happened the way they did, we played a lot better when you came on!'"

"He grabbed me after the match and said, 'You changed the game!' I said, 'I know I changed the game, it was 0-0 when I came on, it was 2-0 for Gillingham soon afterwards!' He said, 'No. You did change the game, if you hadn't have been on there things wouldn't have happened the way they did, we played a lot better when you came on!'

"After the final, I stayed on in London. We'd arranged to meet my old next door neighbour and his wife and we were going out as a foursome with them. The next day though, the Bank Holiday Monday, Paul Dickov was having a barbeque at his house. All the other players had gone up already but I was still in London and I just didn't want to be there anymore. I said to the missus, 'I've got to go. I've got to be with the lads. They're all at Dicky's now, I missed them yesterday, I've got to be with them.' She said, 'go on then.'

"So I legged it down to Euston where there was a 2pm train, I had no ticket, I thought whatever, if the inspector comes I'll just pay on the train and I hopped on with seconds to spare. I had two cans of beer with me, just sat on my own in the seats, not even in a good seat, not even one with table when I noticed people in blue walking by. I realised they were City fans but I was keeping my head down when eventually one of them stopped in front of me. I looked up and it was someone who worked at the ground!

"He said, 'what are you doing here, Bish?' and I said 'I'm off to Dicky's barbeque'. He said, 'There's two carraiges of City fans down there, why don't you give them a wave?' So I just thought, why not, so I went to the bar and brought back two trays of beer and walked into the carriages. They all cheered me and I was handing out the bevvies and in the end I got up on the table and we were all singing City songs all the way back to Manchester. What a brilliant afternoon that was. It's that sort of event which makes me think, 'yeah, you were right to come back.'

"I got off at Stockport and a lad said, 'where are you going, my dad will give you a lift' and so I got a lift to Dicky's house in Bowdon. I could hear all the noise from outside the gates and I shouted "Diiiiicccckkkkkyyyyy!" at the top of my voice over the fence. Immediately, he jumped over and pinned me down in the front garden and for the rest of the day it was great. Everytime I see that goal I always think how brilliant it looks, when he slides across the Wembley turf on his knees in the rain. It was as if it was planned! I was walking round for most of the day with a sausage hanging out of my pants pretending it was something else. You could say we were releasing the stress!"

With the club back in the First Division, Joe and Willie were halfway to their target of back-to-back promotions to the Premiership in two years. It also meant that Bishop was to find the scoresheet again in a game against Port Vale.

"People were saying, he's scored his first goals in ten years for City - it wasn't a surprise. I wasn't here for nine of those years, that's why it took me so long! Strange it wasn't a header. I remember it being 2-0 and I scored both goals and I thought, 'flippin' 'eck, I might be going home with the match ball here,' but I couldn't go looking for that hat-trick, I had to stay disciplined and play for the team! I could have stayed up front but I chose not to.

"As for Blackburn on the last day of the season, well they could have been 5-0 up. They hit the bar about four times. You look at where we'd come from, from Wembley and got up again the following year, it was all down to the hard work we put in from halfway through that season in Division Two. We weren't the second best team that season but we had the momentum and managed to keep it going, we went out thinking, whoever we play we can beat them.

"We all went to the PFA awards the day after Charlton played Ipswich and lost 3-1. We were all in London - all the lads in the pub sweating on the result but Charlton were already up and so perhaps weren't as up for it as Ipswich. We knew then we had to get a result at Blackburn. We knew we had a job to do. It could have gone pear-shaped that day. I nearly died that day. I nearly got trampled on when the fans came on the pitch and I got stuck and people were trying to drag my shirt and shorts off. I heard Spencer Prior had to chin someone to get through - that wouldn't have surprised me anyway. It was great to see the City players and the City fans together, hugging each other in the stands, all singing City anthems. We'd turned the club around together.

"Joe was a lovely, lovely fella, a great fella. I left City at 35 because I was sick of arguing with him about football. I felt that I should be playing, the coaches felt I should be playing, the players said I should be playing and the fans certainly said I should. But Joe wanted Alfie [Haaland] and Ged [Wiekens] - centre halves in midfield. I had no chance."

Former Liverpool man Mike Marsh took the reins of Unibond League side Burscough Town recently and Bishop became his number two, as the pair share the same outlook in life. Although Bishop knows a thing or two about pub management and how hard that is - with its 18-hour days, cleaning glasses, serving food and pulling pints - football is one type of management he is looking to steer well clear from.

"I'll tell you a story. I thought I'd be sick of telling it in my career but it epitomises exactly what I've felt all my career. Willie had some strange ways about him - it was all about the mind, being focused, the psychology of it all. Whenever you hear anybody now, Gerard Houllier especially, 'We were focused today,' I hate that word! Hate it! As if everything is mental, well it's not. The only mental side of it is you being clued up as to how the game should be played and to make sure you don't switch off. Youngsters do it. Seasoned pros do it. Ballwatching happens. To try and impart an important factor to a youngster like jog five yards when the ball's out of play and that'll save you jogging twenty-five yards when it's back in play, getting some of them to understand that and even getting the older pros to keep doing that, sometimes it just goes in one ear and out of the other.

> "Joe [Royle] was a lovely, lovely fella, a great fella. I left City at 35 because I was sick of arguing with him about football. I felt that I should be playing, the coaches felt I should be playing, the players said I should be playing and the fans certainly said I should. But Joe wanted Alfie (Haaland) and Ged (Wiekens) - centre halves in midfield. I had no chance."

"To try and drum that into some of them when they don't want to listen is a really hard job. I've known pros that have played 800 games but they can't put a decent training session on because they just didn't listen, they didn't take anything in. Now if you've played 800 games there's at least 800 weeks when you've trained and they can't put a session on.

"Nowadays they say you need a badge to say you can put a training session on. A schoolteacher can get that badge and get a job before someone who has played 700 odd first team games, which is why I haven't taken a training badge and I never would. It's something I don't agree with. You've got two people there - Howard Wilkinson and Graham Taylor, they're up there saying 'you have to have it' and they've never ever played proper football in their life. I just don't agree with it. If your socks aren't pulled up while you're doing a training course - you fail! It's ridiculous!"

Bishop left Maine Road for the second time and headed off for the glamour of the American League, playing in Miami and having a whale of a time. I put it do him he must have been well into his football, swapping the sights and sounds of South Beach Miami for a rainy night at Frickley Athletic.

"What did I get up to in Miami? Honestly mate, you don't want to know. You really don't want to know! I bought myself a Harley! Turned up for the games on a Harley Davidson. We had a good set of lads, vagabonds, an English manager called Ray Hudson who played for Newcastle and Sunderland so the club had something of an English mentality. I'll probably take the blame for it, the way the lads turned out, but there was me, a South African lad and a lad from New York who were the main ringleaders and we sort of corrupted the young lads and took them out and showed them how it's done in England!

"I'll be totally honest with you, during the two years City got promotion, the lads were having a drink.

It wasn't until we were relegated from the Premier League that it started to become news. According to the press we were getting relegated not because we were playing better teams but because we were having a beer. I saw the reports from the beach in America and I shook my head at the savaging some players were getting. I thought, 'they're my boys.'

"I've got this place for three years but may sell it on in two. I loved it over there and it's only because the club folded that I had to come back. So I may go back to Florida soon. That's the plan, one day I'll go back. But don't get me wrong. City will always be in my heart. I'll always be a Blue."

JOE CORRIGAN
9TH MAY 1981
FA CUP FINAL
CITY 1 TOTTENHAM HOTSPUR 1
ATT : 100,000

The Centenary FA Cup Final of 1981 was arguably the most famous of them all. Alright, there was the White Horse final of 1923 where an estimated 200,000 supporters were present and the Matthews final of 1953 where Blackpool beat Bolton 4-3 and we had the biggest shock of all time when double-chasing Liverpool came unstuck against Wimbledon's Crazy Gang, but for many the two games in '81 added lustre to the 'magic of the cup'.

Yet the Cup has lost some of its sheen of late, whether it be the end of the Monday lunchtime draw or teams withdrawing to jet off to play meaningless tournaments in Brazil, or the apparent disinterest of season ticket holders who don't take up tickets for home games, or even the lure of the Champions League, the tournament has seen better days.

Yet the 1981 final *was* a famous game from an era when the Cup still mattered. Everyone seems to remember it and although even today City fans ponder what might have been, the spectacle and drama concerning those two epic matches has stayed in the memory.

Certainly it has done for Joe Corrigan, City's legendary keeper turned Liverpool goalkeeping coach. He was voted Man of the Match in both games, which is certainly a special feat. City weren't victorious on this occasion but the stature and status of one of the finest goalkeepers this country has ever produced was upheld once again. That's right, 1981 wasn't all about Ricky flippin' Villa!

Joe was too young to feature in the Championship

winning team of 1968 and the FA Cup winning team of 1969. Having made his debut at Blackpool in the League Cup in 1967, he went on to make 476 league appearances for the club and in all competitions he played over 600 times for the Blues - only the great Alan Oakes would play more times. Whilst the Championship was being kept safe in City's trophy cabinet, Corrigan was farmed out to Shrewsbury Town to get some experience and a year later made his full league debut in a 2-1 defeat against Ipswich Town.

He performed heroically in Europe, winning a medal in Vienna in 1970 after playing against Schalke with a broken nose. He also played on with sight in only one eye in a European Cup Winners' Cup tie against Chelsea as well. There was no end to this man's bravery or commitment! Joe won the League Cup twice in 1970 and 1976 but it was Keith MacRae, brought in when Corrigan was going through a troubled period, who kept goal in the 2-1 defeat to Wolves in the 1974 League Cup Final.

So by the time 1981 arrived, Joe, a seasoned campaigner, had never played at Wembley in England's main Cup competition. The fact that this amazing competition was now 100 years old meant the hype surrounding the game hit new heights. It was Bondy's kids against Burkinshaw's men. We all wanted City to win in 1981, but looking back it is truly tragic that Corrigan didn't receive an FA Cup winners medal to go with all his other awards. A true legend like Corrigan deserved it.

The Joe Corrigan story began in Alderley Road in Sale Moor and there's one thing about Joe you may find surprising. Corrigan, a name that immediately conjures up memories of City's glory days, was actually a United supporter as a youngster and might have signed for Matt Busby had The Citizens not stepped in as quickly as they did.

"I'm not so sure these days but certainly back then Sale was more of a red area and my uncle was a fanatical Manchester United supporter. So I chose United simply because of him. I always used to play in goal in the parks around my home and for a local team called AEI. One day I went to work and I was told that a Manchester City scout wanted me to come down for a trial. It was Harry Godwin, the famous chief scout who'd brought so many players to the club. Apparently he told Joe Mercer that I'd either be a clown or a classic! Sometimes I wonder if I was the former! Nevertheless, they must have liked what they saw as they signed me up after just one training session. Manchester United enquired about me just two weeks later but they were too late - I was already contracted to City. City had shown faith in me and I wanted to carve out a career in professional football.

"The first thing I noticed about City when I arrived were the traditions of the club. Especially being a goalkeeper because all the other players who have worn the No 1 jersey are aware of the history of people like Frank Swift and Bert Trautmann. You feel quite daunted by it. City have always had good goalkeepers and I felt I had a lot to live up to. Later on, people were trying to compare me with the likes of Big Swifty and Bert but I never wanted that. I wanted to say, 'I'm not the second Frank Swift, I'm the first Joe Corrigan'."

Naturally, people are going to look at the history books and scan some of the names that have played in goal for City. As well as Bert and Frank there was Harry Dowd and Ken Mulhearn. Tony Coton, who was idolised by the City fans for five or six years until he joined United, Peter Schmeichel and David Seaman are keepers who reached the very top of their profession, but only signed short-term contracts with the club. Corrigan was different because he stayed at City for so long and that immediately means he gets bracketed with the likes of Swift and Trautmann in the file stamped 'Legend Material'.

Joe's early career saw those two triumphs in the 1969-70 season and he might have been forgiven for thinking football was always going to be like this. It wasn't of course, there was a lot of hard work along the way and for a spell Joe well and truly hit the doldrums. A battle with confidence and weight together with some concentration problems meant Keith MacRae became City's No 1 at one stage. Manager Ron Saunders placed Corrigan on the transfer list and almost immediately Joe became motivated again. It is an experience that means he can pass on heartfelt advice to the goalkeepers he works with at Melwood training ground every morning.

People remember the times when he was caught cold. Such was City's attacking prowess that Corrigan used to go for long periods during a game without having to touch the ball.

BELOW: Joe's recovery, following a transfer listing under Ron Saunders, led to a call-up to the naitonal squad.

One such occasion was when Ronnie Boyce lobbed him from the halfway line during a terrible 5-1 home defeat against West Ham in 1971. Thankfully, those painful memories became something of a character building exercise and Joe took his 6 foot 4 inch frame to the gym in an attempt to get fitter and re-focus. The rewards came at national level with nine England caps and he was voted Supporters' Player of the Year in 1979. It is to Joe's eternal credit that he turned his career around.

As he says, "The West Ham game was well documented at the time but I never felt I was a bad keeper or anything. I put it down to a learning curve. That's football, it was just one of those things."

Parallels can perhaps be drawn with David James' career. James went through a spell of making unforced errors that he later put down to concentration difficulties. He blamed his habit of playing computer games and being a goalkeeper, his mistakes were magnified more than his outfield counterparts. Thanks to Joe's help and dedication, James regained his form and went on to play for England witrh great distinction.

"It was always an honour for me to play for Manchester City and I played in two great teams. In the late 60s and early 70s and then that second team between 1976 and 1979. The only difference in my eyes between these two superb teams, the reason why one side won one League Cup and the other won everything, was because Colin Bell was injured and you know, Colin Bell was simply irreplaceable. We missed that player in midfield who could get us 20 goals a season. I'm totally convinced looking back that, had he been available, we'd have finished 1st not 2nd and 4th."

After the League Cup triumph in 1976 came Joe's England debut against Italy. Things were going well again, Joe's City career had already seen more ups and downs than the FTSE 100 Index! After a difficult period when Malcolm Allison returned, City produced two cup runs out of nothing in 1981. The League Cup chase ran out of steam in the semis, but the FA Cup train went all the way to Wembley.

"We finished the league season on the Saturday and on the Wednesday beforehand we travelled down to the Salisden Park Hotel. We went there in '76. In '74 we stayed at Champneys Health club in Tring which was very relaxing and in '70 we stayed at The

Grosvenor Hotel. That's one good thing about being a footballer and making finals - you stay in some good hotels!

"There was no doubt in the press that we were the underdogs but John Bond noticed what was being written and used these comments as a motivational tool for us. He was a good motivator, was Bondy and he fostered a good spirit amongst the lads, morale was sky high and with the blending in of the three new signings: Gow, Hutchison and McDonald, together with kids like Tommy Caton, Tony Henry and Nicky Reid who'd made their mark in the season - the belief was back once again. We had a good balance. John kept the build-up quite low key really, he tried to prepare us in the normal way but there was still something a bit different about that week. You felt different. Yet we weren't fazed by the occasion in any way, by the time we were striding out down the tunnel we were just concentrating on those eleven players.

"Looking back, and this is not sour grapes by the way, I don't believe any final should be settled by a replay. I'd say the same thing even if we'd won. The players, the fans, everyone, we got so built up for the day, you just want to see it settled on the day. I genuinely feel that going to a replay is the wrong way to settle it, it should be all done and dusted on the day.

"We played so well on the Saturday, we were eight minutes away from winning the Cup. Their goal was a complete fluke and it came right out of the blue. Even in extra time we still had the best of the play, we were the better team. Tottenham's legs had gone but we just couldn't find that winner. At the end of 120 minutes it should've gone to penalties or continued until we had a

"I played in two great teams. The only difference in my eyes between these 2 superb teams, the reason why one side won one League Cup and the other won everything, was because Colin Bell was injured and you know, Colin Bell was simply irreplaceable."

golden goal because you're worked up and like I say, you like to see it resolved on the day - a day when it truly feels like Cup Final day.

"The goal, well I can remember it as if it were yesterday. We'd been practising defending free kicks all week and John Bond wanted to place an extra man on the line just to give us that extra protection. The team talked about it between themselves and decided against the idea. So on the day I was setting up the wall, Tommy Hutchison, who remember had scored a great goal for us in the first half, was in the wall and broke away because he'd heard what the Spurs players were planning and he knew what they were going to do.

"So he decided to move to counteract this. Tommy was trying to do his best for the team of course but the free kick just rebounded off him - square off his shoulder and past me into the net. We were sickened, it was heartbreaking to lead for so long and not win. We were down but we had to pick ourselves up immediately, which to be fair... we did.

"Walking down the tunnel after the game I felt like we'd lost. We were still in the competition but I felt we'd let a great opportunity slip through our fingers. You can't blame Tommy though - it was just one of those things."

The 1-1 draw meant a replay in the final for the first time since Chelsea played Leeds in 1970. On the Saturday Ricky Villa had been jeered off by the City fans when he was substituted. He was to exact his own devastating revenge.

"As for the replay, well firstly the tickets went on sale at Wembley on the Sunday morning after most of our

> **"The goal, well I can remember it as if it were yesterday. We'd been practising defending freekicks all week and John Bond wanted to place an extra man on the line... [Tommy] broke away because he'd heard what the Spurs players were planning... it came square off his shoulder and past me into the net"**

supporters had returned home. We only had about 26,000 there for the replay out of 92,500 which in itself is another reason why the replay was unfair. The allocations in the first game were 50-50.

"Every year the Villa goal is shown on television. Fair play to the lad, he took his goal well but in my opinion it wasn't a great goal. We were tired, our defending was a shambles and we should have cleared it before he put it away. But it was the winner and that's why it was remembered. Steve McKenzie's goal was much better but no-one remembers it, because it wasn't the winner."

City came from behind to lead 2-1 in the replay before Garth Crooks and Ricky Villa came back to steal the cup for Spurs. The Cup, which City had had one hand on for most of Saturday and some of

the replay, was lost. Corrigan left City when John Bond walked in 1983, to pursue a career in Seattle, bringing to an end an association with City that had lasted for nearly two decades. He may be at the wrong end of the East Lancs Road currently but he should have no doubt that Joe Corrigan's place is secure in the Manchester City hall of fame.

KEN BARNES
7ᵀᴴ DECEMBER 1957
FIRST DIVISION
CITY 6 EVERTON 2
ATT: 20,912

I'm on my way to Platt Lane training ground to meet Ken Barnes. Once a week the 'old boys' meet up for a cup of tea and a chat about all things City. There's Fred Eyre, Johnny Williamson, Stevie Fleet and Ken himself. They're the mainstays of these get-togethers although a host of other former players and coaches tend to drop in for a natter. It's a meeting of the minds and, having been able to eavesdrop on their conversation, it makes me wish Ken was still involved at City in some shape of form. Yet I feel like I'm intruding on something very private before Ken's lovely smile and welcoming grin eases my mind.

The game that has lived longest in Ken's memory was the occasion he scored a hat-trick of penalties in one game. This was during City's 6-2 defeat of Everton at Maine Road. It was something of an overcast, blustery day and in that era all the season ticket holders were seated in the Main Stand. I wonder how many supporters opened their curtains that morning and thought, 'I'll give it a miss today'. Christmas shopping may not have been the hectic occasion it is today and there was always the appeal of an open fire and the wireless but there were only 21,000 present for a game where history was made, which is surprising considering the goal feast that City were enjoying at the time.

Prior to kick off City were tenth and Everton were two places higher

> **"The funniest was when the third penalty was awarded... I'd made eye contact with the Everton 'keeper, Albert Dunlop, and knowing I'd beaten him twice in both corners I said 'Albert, you've no flippin' chance with this one!' and he laughed back!"**

82

in eighth. Yet though this was something of a mid-table clash, City were going into their 20th game of the season having scored 52 and conceded 51! Even by typical City standards, the inconsistency was becoming ridiculous!

"I was the regular penalty taker for City, but you don't expect to score 3 in one game!" laughs Ken, "certainly I think it's been done once or maybe twice but the people who have done it have all died - I think I'm the only one that's done it that's still alive! I know Anelka scored two for City against Villa recently but that's the nearest anyone has come.

"My recollection of the game is hazy these days. It was nearly 50 years ago but I think all the penalties came at the Platt Lane End in the second half. I can't recall how the penalties were won either but I'm pretty sure Sanders, their full back, was responsible for two of them.

"Now when I took a penalty I'd usually put them to the left of the keeper. Just side-foot them into the corner and when we were awarded our first penalty that's exactly what I did. I stroked it into the usual place.

"Then we were awarded the second spot kick so immediately I had a dilemma. Shall I put it in the usual place or try the other corner? I walked up and put the ball on the spot and as I was doing this I still hadn't decided which way to go. I ran up and at the last second before striking the ball I decided to place it to the keeper's right, the opposite side and in it went.

"The funniest was when the third penalty was awarded. The whole ground howled with laughter as they knew it gave me the chance to complete a unique hat-trick. I'd made eye contact with the Everton keeper, Albert Dunlop, and knowing I'd beaten him twice in both corners I said, 'Albert, you've no flippin' chance with this one!' and he laughed back! This time I returned to the normal place and in it went for my hat-trick."

City had lined up that afternoon with Trautmann in goal and a back five of Ken himself, Cliff Sear, Roy Warhurst, Dave Ewing and Bill Leivers. The forward five were Joey Hayes, Bobby Johnstone, Bill McAdams, Colin Barlow and Roy Clarke. Many of the starting XI had featured in the glory of the Wembley Cup runs but City seemed to be moving into something of a transitional period, despite the fact this win moved them up to the heady heights of fifth place. For fans and players alike, the season seemed to involve one step forward and one back. 104 goals were scored and 100 conceded in the League this season.

BELOW:
Ken celebrates victory in the 1956 FA Cup Final with a fag and some champers.

"We had some big wins and some big defeats in 1957-58. The big defeats you remember more because they hurt more. We weren't over-attacking, it's not that we didn't care about defensive duties, of course we did. It's just the way the game was played in those days. We went out to win the game, to entertain the public - defenders defended and forwards attacked. None of this all-back-at-corners routine or man-marking nonsense.

"Football has changed over the years. Today it's very tactical. We don't see the same number of good wingers around, or if we do, we see them being

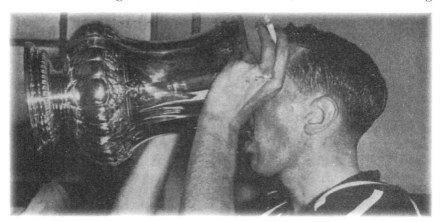

accommodated at wing-back. One day I was walking through the corridors at Maine Road and Bill Shankly said, 'You've got a good 'un there in your lad Peter,' and I replied, 'Aye, he's got a chance.' 'Got a chance?' said Shankly, 'he's brilliant but he shouldn't be having to run 80 yards before getting the ball in, he'll be burnt out!' and I agreed with him - the game needs width and wingers and you should always look for a win, not sit back on a 1-0 lead. Even from 1957 to 1966 the game evolved because we won the World Cup playing with no wingers. They were Alf Ramsey's 'wingless wonders', weren't they."

Yet in 1957 the game was still based on the simple W and M formations that had dominated the game since the 1930s. This formation looks bizarre today, as it typically featured five attackers, a formation reserved today for fighting lost causes!

"What I remember about that day in particular was that it was very blustery. Conditions were poor and the pitch wasn't as good as it was in Stan Gibson's day. People were missing challenges and that's possibly why those penalties were awarded, because the tackles were flying in.

"Roy Paul had left for Worcester City and Roy Warhurst, who played at Wembley in '56 came in, so that was the only major change at the back. He had guile and was a true leader, was Roy Paul, it was difficult to replace someone like that. Big Dave Ewing was still there and he'd get stuck in, he was hard but fair. Their centre-forward Dave Hickson fouled Ewing all the way through the game and it was going on

ABOVE:
One of the finest full-backs of his generation, Barnes was once described as 'the best uncapped defender who ever played in English football'.

behind the referee's back.

"Finally Dave got fed up and booted Hickson right up the backside, much to the amusement of the crowd. It was a man's game then. There'd be good hard tussles all over the park and if it was one man marking one man you'd have to win your battle. Dave wasn't a dirty player and I suppose Hickson, who was a determined character, and Everton generally were frustrated by what had happened that day."

A lot of able attackers used to be stopped in the tracks by Ken Barnes in his hey day - a dependable wing half and City legend.

MARK LILLIS
21ˢᵀ AUG 1985
FIRST DIVISION
CITY 1 LEICESTER CITY 1
ATT: 25,528

Everybody who makes it into the world of professional football starts out with the clichéd schoolboy dream of making it big. It may have started in the park with your mates, in a street or an alleyway as your imagination takes you from kicking a ball against the wall to playing in the World Cup for England or scoring the winner in a cup final at Wembley. So it was with Mark Lillis.

Then again Lillis actually did score a hat-trick in a Cup Final at Wembley. Well, he did, until some jobsworth decided one of them was actually a Doug Rougvie own goal, but even so, this amazing feat didn't provide him with his proudest moment of his football life. No, Mark Lillis' favourite game was the night he made his home debut for the team he has always supported.

You'd be pushed to find this game in any history books on City and it's unlikely to be featured on any end of an era video or DVD. However Manchester City's tame 1-1 draw Leicester City at Maine Road in August 1985 gave Lillis the chance to finally run down that famous tunnel in front of all his mates in the Kippax in the sky blue of City and from the moment he could first kick a ball in anger that's all he ever wanted to do.

It's not easy to forget Mark Lillis. The extravagant goal celebrations, the shoulder length blond hair, and of course, the stunning fightback against Chelsea in the inaugural Full Members' Cup Final - a 5-4 defeat in a short-lived competition that most fans seemed loath to support until the final itself.

A proud Mancunian, Lillis was an immensely popular

player who topped City's scoring charts in a difficult season - 1985-86. He went to manage and coach, yet even today he lives and breathes Manchester City and, until recently, was assistant to Sammy McIlroy in the Northern Ireland set-up.

Mark has always been a blue and was brought up with the City traditions from an early age. "I was born at St Mary's Hospital and I was originally brought up in Longsight, attending St Robert's Primary school and then I moved onto St Mark's Barlow High, the same school as Noel and Liam Gallagher!"

Unlike the famous Burnage boys, Lillis actually fulfilled his childhood ambition of playing up front for City at Wembley. Noel and Liam had to make do with kicking a ball about on Cringle Fields - oh and entertaining 250,000 people at Knebworth. "Just shows what a talented school it was - me and Oasis," laughs Lillis.

"After that I moved down to Wythenshawe and Brooklands - my family are all Blues and they live in Brooklands near Sale. I've been a City fan all my life. I signed schoolboy forms at 14 but I was rejected by Tony Book at 16. That was hard to take. I was gutted really. At the time City couldn't make up their minds whether they wanted to keep me or not - they hadn't said yes, they hadn't said no but they were keeping me waiting. My dad went in and told them that he was pulling me out of the club. I was sat in a car outside Maine Road at the time absolutely devastated. So from there I went for trials everywhere: Burnley, Bury, Chester, Sheffield Wednesday. Just when I was leaving school I was weighing up my options, football or some other trade like electrician. One of my best mates, even now, is Martin Arthurs, Bonehead's brother. He was going into that field when all of a sudden I got the call from Huddersfield Town and it all started again. My dad's gut feeling was that if City weren't sure they wanted me I should leave for a lower league club and if I was good enough eventually things would come round full circle. He was absolutely right!"

That early rejection moulded some toughness into Lillis' character. You couldn't keep him down for long and even today in his coaching career he's experienced his fair share of clubs.

"I'd captained Manchester Boys from Under-11 to Under-16 and I was a centre-half really. It was only under Mick Buxton at Huddersfield that he pitched me in up-front against Reading and when I started scoring we knew it was the position for me. At that time, though, I thought my chance of playing for City had gone forever, but we did very well at Huddersfield. We gained promotion from the old Fourth Division to the old Second Division. We came back to Maine Road and won 3-2, even though Kevin Bond scored with two dubious penalties for City!"

Lillis was making great progress with the Terriers and even today remains one of their fans' all-time heroes. Billy McNeill also took notice and asked Huddersfield for permission to speak with him.

"It was a done deal almost as soon as I'd heard of City's interest although I could have gone to Chelsea or West Ham as well. I'd have regretted it though had I not signed for City as it was my boyhood ambition. I'd had my first chance taken away from me, so I really didn't want this opportunity to slip through my fingers either.

"So me and the wife met Billy McNeill and Freddie Pye down at the Post House in Northenden. Freddie knew of other clubs that were in for me and probably also realised that my wages at Huddersfield weren't at all brilliant, so during negotiations he asked me if there was anything he could do for me. Almost immediately my wife piped up, 'We've been scrimping and saving for six months to get a new carpet for the bedroom.' Freddie saw his chance and said, 'If Mark signs for City, I'll pay for the whole house to be carpeted!'

"So I went along to this place in Cheetham Hill, it wasn't what you'd call a modern superstore or anything like that, but he'd written this address out on a piece of paper for me and I pushed this door open and this well-built shaven-headed bloke with tattoos all over his arms bounded over to me! I said, 'I've just signed for City and I've come for my carpets' and this guy pointed at a rail of carpets that I could choose from! Obviously what with agents and all that, deals are a bit different these days!"

City offered more than just carpets though. They stumped up £132,500 after a tribunal for the player they needed to spearhead their return to Division One. With Lillis back at his spiritual home and The Blues back in the top flight, it was with great excitement that Lillis looked forward to the opening game of the season - Coventry City at Highfield Road.

"What I remember about that day is that there was a massive turn out from the City fans behind the goal. It looked like there were 10,000 plus there. Alright, the records may show there were less present but that's how it seemed to me. Seeing that huge following and knowing all those people were there to support you, it just spurs you on. Sammy Mac scored his only goal for City that day in a 1-1 draw.

"Me and Sammy signed on the same day, 7th August 1985 and while it was well known I had City connections, it was also well known about Sammy's United past. Sammy though had no problem about playing for City and to be fair he was stitched up by a newspaper reporter at an early stage and the situation was allowed to fester.

"He gave an interview and the reporter then added some comments like 'I still prefer United to City even though I play for City' and not surprisingly, the fans didn't like those comments and took it out on him, but he never actually said that and that was the problem.

"We had a team meeting about it six weeks after

OPPOSITE:
The sight of
Mark Lillis
attacking
the visitor's
goal excited
the Kippax
during the
mid-80s.

it had come out and I stuck up for Sammy because someone at the club had sanctioned the interview and must've checked it before it had gone to print but weren't owning up to it. They certainly weren't prepared to defend Sammy in the press. Billy Mac said he'd investigate it but we never found out who was responsible so of course nothing changed. But Sammy bears no ill feeling towards the City fans - in fact he feels that if the article had never been done it might have been a different story and he might have built a relationship with the City fans. People have played for both sides before - Peter Barnes went to United and we had Brian Kidd and Peter Schmeichel at City. The City fans gave great backing to those two so it was a real shame that only Sammy has missed out. I hooked up with Sammy at Macclesfield as assistant for a time so yeah, we go back a long way. Now I'm doing the Northern Ireland job which is a tremendous honour, to pit your wits against teams and managers at international level."

Next up was Leicester City at Maine Road... Lillis couldn't wait. "The buzz of making my home debut was incredible. It was emotional for me. I was having a kick about on the pitch and I looked up at my dad and some other family members who have sadly passed away since but they all gave me a wave and my dad was giving me the clenched fist sign.

"I used to stand on the Kippax watching all my heroes: Bell, Lee, Summerbee, Alan Oakes, Neil Young... and here I was in possession of a blue shirt. I wasn't going to let anyone take it away from me.

"I remember the build-up to the goal. I think I crossed it into the box for Gordon Davies and there was a handball. So I picked up the ball and put it on the spot. Then, as I was walking backwards, I was thinking, 'where should I put it?' I thought my family, my mum, dad and uncles are in the Main Stand to my left and all my mates were over to my right in the Kippax. There was no way I was going to miss it and I tucked it away and sprinted over Linford Christie-style to the Kippax to give the fans a bit of a jig. This was my moment and I intended to enjoy it! I climbed up the perimeter fencing saluting the City fans. I was going absolutely mental. This went on for a few seconds, then elation turned into acute awareness - I turned around to see who was celebrating with me but there was no-one near me at all! I then realised I had to retake the penalty, which fortunately I scored with again. This time though, there was no celebration, I just walked back to the centre circle shaking the odd hand because I was absolutely goosed! I thought I've finally done it. I've actually scored for City on my debut. We didn't win but I was ecstatic. No one can ever take that goal away from me and I went out for a few scoops to celebrate."

After early successes against West Brom and Tottenham, the Blues slipped

> **"During negotiations he asked me if there was anything he could do for me and almost immediately my wife piped up, 'We've been scrimping and saving for six months to get a new carpet for the bedroom' - Freddie saw his chance and said 'If Mark signs for City, I'll pay for the whole house to be carpeted!'"**

alarmingly down the table. The fans were looking at a long, hard winter. Many teams could have crumbled in that scenario but from somewhere City picked up a 2-0 win at Forest and then found a run of results to push them right up the table. As well as having some good players, the team spirit and morale amongst the lads was second to none.

"Looking back, Billy McNeill didn't do that much in the way of taking us for training. He left that to other people, or more often than not - us the players! Me and Neil McNab, for instance, developed that cheeky free kick routine where he'd look up and gesticulate, then I'd make a quick run and disrupt the markers and he could then float it in. So it was good to have that freedom. What also helped was that a lot of the lads in the side were Mancunians. In the Manchester derbies that year, about 8 of the 11 in our team were from Manchester, with Peter Barnes the only one in their team and even he was an ex-Blue!

"What I'm saying is that there was good banter in the dressing room which is what you need when you're up against it. I was sometimes the centre of attention, in fact, even to this day managers in the game when they phone me up call me 'Bhuna'! After each home game I'd go to Cellar Vie in town, off Albert Square or head for the Sandpiper, now called Robinski's opposite the Queen of Hearts in Fallowfield. These were the big haunts for City players.

"After a quick drink I'd always go for a Chicken Bhuna! Without fail! Every week! I love Indian food and I still have to have my fix of Bhuna at the weekend. It became something of a standing joke on a Monday morning. We'd turn up for training and everybody would be discussing where they went over the weekend. Some of them would've gone to some poncy wine bar or a fancy club or even a posh meal with their wives or girlfriends. Then it'd come round to me. 'What did you do Mark?' 'Just went for a Chicken Bhuna!' 'What again?' 'Yeah, why, what's wrong with that?'

"I think the only time when I didn't go out was when we lost 3-1 to Watford in the Cup replay at Maine Road. I think I missed a penalty, but to be fair, that night was the John Barnes show and he took us apart. I was so gutted though, I didn't go out of the house for a week, so looking back I must've missed out on my Bhuna!"

As winter turned into spring, City were looking at a much healthier mid-table position, allowing them to blood promising youngsters such as Stevie Redmond. During this spell, Lillis notched some vital goals, putting some daylight between City and the relegation zone.

"I remember scoring the winner at Villa and I spent some time, shall we say, saluting the City fans. Mick McCarthy, who these days is a massive Blue, tried to rollock me saying what I was doing was unprofessional. I said, 'I don't care. City is my club and I'm proud to wear this shirt. I'm celebrating with my fans.' If I wasn't a player, I'd have been in amongst them in the Witton End watching the game."

Wembley that year came in the form of the Full Members Cup, forerunner of the Simod Cup and the Zenith Data Systems Cup. It was one cup too many maybe in an already hectic football schedule.

"To be honest, we didn't really think about the final until after the derby. We'd made a brilliant comeback with Clive Wilson's diving header and we were all pretty pleased with the outcome after being 2-0 down. We boarded the coach at Old Trafford and we headed straight to the hotel in London.

"Billy Mac was at the front of the coach and he was having a couple of drinks, we could see this and we fancied a bit of the same. We only wanted one or two back at the hotel to loosen down after the derby so I enquired on behalf of the lads but Billy just snarled, 'What do you think youse are, a pub team or something!' So I tried to explain I was only asking on behalf of 'the lads', but when I turned round to look for support, 'the lads' were all ducking and diving for cover under their chairs and wouldn't say a word! So sheepishly I retreated, Billy had his beer and me and Neil McNab, who I used to room with, we just made do with a brew in the hotel room and talked about the derby, then we just went to sleep.

"There was a lot of talk in the press about how the turn out was going to be so low but 70,000 wasn't a bad gate, was it, and it was a final, so in that respect the competition was worth winning. Steve Kinsey put us ahead early on but then it went 1-1, 2-1, 3-1 4-1 and then 5-1. At 5-1 I was lining up to take the centre thinking, 'I can't possibly show my face in Manchester ever again - we've got to get back into this' so we just went for it.

"About the same time Paul Simpson came on as a sub and it changed the game. I fed it out to Simmo who took it down the left and swung it in, I got on the end of his cross and headed it in - 5-2. Then I think Andy May was fouled and I scored the penalty. Then I had a goal disallowed and then we made it 5-4. So I thought I'd scored a hat-trick and I thought, God, we've got these cockneys on the rack here, another 3 or 4 minutes and we'll win this 6-5. Then almost immediately the referee blew the whistle for time and it was a complete anticlimax. We'd recovered some pride and made a game out of it at least. That night we all had a meal together at Maine Road but it just fizzled out into a complete anticlimax, made even worse when the third goal was later taken off me."

The following season gave Lillis hope of becoming City's captain. Little did he know that he was soon to be shown the exit door. "Pre-season in 1986 we went

"I was going absolutely mental. This went on for a few seconds, then elation turned into acute awareness - I turned around to see who was celebrating with me but there was no-one near me at all! I then realised I had to retake the penalty, which fortunately I scored with again"

on a trip to Switzerland. Me, Kenny Clements and Mick McCarthy were all given the captain's armband for one game. When I was captain we won our game 1-0. I really did think the armband was up for grabs and McNeill must have contemplated it.

"When we came back though he told me he'd accepted an offer from Derby County because the club was skint and would I talk to them. Well I never wanted to go, not in a million years, but my attitude was still that of a fan. I agreed to go simply because I thought by leaving I'd be helping City ease their financial burden, you know, I'd be doing the club a favour! So it was a real wrench to go. Obviously, I was back home in Manchester and it meant uprooting again but I wouldn't have swapped that year for anything and I can safely say I've not looked back since. I think a lot of things are down to fate. I went to Derby and Villa and hooked up with John Gregory and ended up working with him as reserve team manager."

I suggest Mark's career recalls the old joke that Tommy Docherty used to make about more clubs than Jack Nicklaus. "I won a Second Division championship medal with Villa under Graham Taylor and in '88 we went to Maine Road and won. I got a great reception from the City fans and that brought a lump to my throat. Round about this time though I started to pick up a few injuries so I started thinking seriously about coaching. I went to Scunthorpe and then Stockport County under Danny Bergara and eventually started coaching the youth team back at Huddersfield under Brian Horton. My job was to nurture the players and bring them through. One of these was Andy Booth, who went to Sheffield Wednesday for £3 million.

> **"Soon after arriving at Derby I took the training and I started singing 'Blue Moon' at Kinkladze, who just looked at me as if I was off my head! He didn't know I'd played for City before him but we stayed behind kicking the ball about talking about City. We'd both moved on but we hadn't as well, if you like."**

"Later I became caretaker manager at Scunthorpe and then became head coach there under Brian Laws. We won the Third Division play-off final and then I took up the manager's job at Halifax Town for 14 months. I was actually manager of Halifax when they played City in a pre-season friendly and I told the stadium announcer to wish City all the best for the season!

"Football is a crazy game and I was feeling low, really low when I got the bullet from Halifax. I was driving home in the rain on a cold, dark, Tuesday night and by the Saturday I'd started scouting for Aston Villa for Premiership and European games. It was a bright sunny day on the Saturday and I was sat up in the directors' box at Anfield watching a brilliant game thinking, Christ, this is a bit different to Halifax!

"Soon after arriving at Derby I took the training and I started singing *Blue Moon* at Kinkladze, who just looked at me as if I was off my head! He didn't know I'd played for City before him but we stayed behind kicking the ball about talking about City. We'd both moved on but we hadn't as well, if you like. I enjoyed working with Kinky, he's got some great talent but I'm still not sure what his best position is.

"As I've said, I've done a lot of scouting since and as a scout you're supposed to remain impartial but I took my dad along to the City - Everton game in 2000 that City won 5-0. When City scored we jumped up in the directors box and we were told in no uncertain terms by another club's scout, who I won't name, that we couldn't do that. So when we went 2-0 up I made a point of leaping up again and cheering for even longer. I turned round to him and said, 'Sorry mate. I'm a scout but I'm also a Blue!'"

Just goes to show, you can take the boy out of City, but you can't take City out of the boy.

PADDY FAGAN
12ᵀᴴ FEBRUARY 1955
FIRST DIVISION
MANCHESTER UNITED 0 CITY 5
ATT: 47,914

A skilful Irishman terrorising the Manchester United defence. No, it's not Niall Quinn or even Mark Kennedy - Paddy Fagan was the man who wrote himself into Manchester City history back in February 1955 on a day when the Mighty Blues tore the famous Busby Babes to shreds. Many younger City fans may not know too much about Paddy Fagan but he was an important member of the side back in the fifties and played in the 1955 FA Cup Final, which City sadly lost to a Jackie Milburn inspired Newcastle United.

In this game he was the scourge of the United back-line - scoring twice in that 5-0 rout, with the other goals coming from Johnny Hart and two from Joey Hayes. Paddy also scored an important goal in the other league derby that season, a 3-2 win for City at Maine Road, on a day where Hart again and Billy McAdams also found the back of the net. In fact, the fourth round FA Cup tie between Manchester's big two on January 29th 1955 saw City see off United to the tune of two goals to nil. Three times that season the old foes clashed and on all three occasions the Sky Blues came out on top.

In fact City won five derbies out of six in that era, the other being a 1-1 draw in January 1954. United's team were gaining recognition but in derbies City were more than matching them. It is well known that the team Manchester United lost in 1958 were an exceptionally gifted young side, so it must say something about the quality of the City team that they performed so well in those head-to-head encounters.

Paddy's first name is really Fionan and he only

picked up the nickname Paddy because of his broad
Dublin accent. Fagan is a Gaelic name and means
'little fiery one' and certainly at Wembley in 1955,
when the chips were down and City were a man down,
no-one tried harder to turn the situation around
than Paddy Fagan. He never gave up.

A full international for the Republic of Ireland,
Paddy won eight full caps and played five more as
substitute. During his City career he scored 34 league
goals in 153 matches, a respectable enough tally for a
winger. But it is his performance in the 5-0 humiliation
of United at Old Trafford that places him in the hearts
of City die-hards. "I played in the three derby wins
that season - I got a couple of goals over them in the
5-0. I don't remember too much about them, how they
went in, but I do know at the time they were ruling
the roost in Manchester, the Busby Babes. They were
the team of the future and if it happened nowadays
everyone would sit up and take notice. Well, let me tell
you, it had the same impact back then.

"I'm not saying they were a bad side, they weren't,
they were a very good side, but we had a good side too.
I'd say the teams were very equal. They had Duncan
Edwards, Colin Webster, Jackie Blanchflower, Roger
Byrne - but we had a good side, Jimmy Meadows, Ken
Barnes, Roy Little, Roy Paul, Bobby Johnstone, Don
Revie. We played to our strengths and the formation
we adopted suited us - it was done that way to make it
to our advantage. We went out to play a formation and
we had to let the opposing team counteract it. It was
no good us going out there thinking 'we're playing
such and such a team today, we've got to change our
formation' - we'd never have won!

"The other team was to worry about us, not us
about them. We kept the ball and had the players
to do this. Ken Barnes was the best wing half in the
country and we had Bobby Johnstone, a great player.
Don Revie was a great passer of the ball, Roy Paul was

ABOVE:
Destroyer of
United in
1955, Paddy
went on to
win 8 caps for
Eire.

a marvellous man to have as captain. And I felt I had two good feet, that was my strength. I could play outside-left or outside-right and I actually did both at Wembley. What I am saying then is that our success was not down to individual brilliance - it was because we played as a team.

"When we came off the pitch we were elated because beating United by such a score doesn't happen that often, especially on their own ground but at the same time, over the years when I was at City, we played other teams and were beaten by big scores. 8-4 at Leicester, 9-2 at West Brom and Preston beat us 5-0."

One such amazing but perhaps typical game of that era was a game in 1957 when Manchester City drew Newcastle United in the FA Cup. A 1-1 draw on Tyneside meant a replay four days later that became something of a goal feast. The Geordies won by the odd goal in nine but it should never be forgotten that City were actually 3-0 up in this game after just 25 minutes. 3-0 it stayed until half time and in the second half the Blues were quickly pegged back to 3-2. A late equaliser meant a 3-3 draw after 90 minutes and extra time beckoned. By now Newcastle had the momentum and the belief but amazingly, City went back in front. Yet there was still time for Newcastle to storm back and pinch the game 5-4! In 1957-58 City scored 104 goals yet conceded 100! If their defence had been a bit tighter, perhaps they might have given Wolves a stronger run for their money at the top of the league. In Paddy's view, the fact City scored and conceded in such equal measure was simply typical of that time.

"I scored in that Newcastle cup game and we were

3-0 up at half time. We lost 5-4! My explanation? Well, it was just one of those things. The team just collapsed. You can't put your finger on why it happened, it just happened! This is the beauty of the game, this is what football is like. If you could predict football, you'd win the pools every week. It was just down to them taking their chances. They didn't get many but the ones they got they put away. That's just the way it is. Every time they got a chance - Bang! It was a goal! We went in at 3-0 and I suppose we lost our concentration. It was just a matter of going out for 45 minutes and coming in with the game closed off and won. In those days, we had an attacking formation, all the forwards would go and get the goals and it would be simply down to the defenders to do the defending. At least we did our job that day. My most consistent period was between 1954 and 1956. I had a licence to stay forward. For a wing man I got quite a lot of goals."

Talking to Paddy it's quite apparent how football and tactics have changed over the last 50 years. "I had a position to play, which was to stay up front, that was accepted as my role. I wasn't to drop back or anything like that. I had a position just like everyone else had a position and I might drop inside or simply go up and down depending on the opposition. It was a very simple game then and things have changed since then.

"I only played four games the following season, 1955-56, because of injury. I was out for the whole season. I missed the Cup Final victory over Birmingham but I felt I'd played my part in the previous year's cup run. Missing the 1956 Final was just one of those things. I was disappointed that I couldn't play but I just wanted the boys to win - I wished them all the best. You've got to accept the bonuses and the

"It was no good us going out there thinking 'we're playing such and such a team today, we've got to change our formation' - we'd never have won!"

disappointments also. Everything can't be on the up all the time, you've got to remain placid over these things."

Paddy had arrived at City three years previously and was something of a young starlet, perhaps the Damien Duff of his era!

"I was born in Dublin and I was brought over to England by Raich Carter who was a very famous England international and player-manager of Hull City. So I signed professional forms and then transferred to Manchester City on Christmas Eve 1953 and by Christmas Day I was playing in the reserves and by Boxing Day I was in the first team against Sheffield United.

"I think we won but I was at City sixd years before signing for Derby County. It was Les McDowall who'd brought me to City. I didn't know anything about it before I got into the Hull team. There were rumours and speculation that I was going to go to Newcastle in the Hull papers and it was said Hull had refused a £15,000 fee for someone who hadn't played in the first team yet."

"Football's changed really. For a 17-year-old it was a very big fee but they must have thought we'll hang onto him and see if he's any good for us. Then the new manager came in and he had different ideas and we parted company. More than anything we didn't see eye-to-eye. So I came over to Manchester to see Les McDowall the manager and I signed for him right away. I got on well with Les McDowall. I think Les McDowall was quite well educated and you couldn't pull the wool over his eyes, but he knew his footballers. We didn't see eye to eye on everything but we did get on pretty well whilst he was manager. As he was leaving, George Poyser came in as manager, he was Les' assistant manager for a while with the proviso that he would be a manager eventually. He was a nice enough man but I didn't think he had management qualities - well in fact we got relegated under George Poyser so there you go! I didn't think he was the right man for the job of manager of a big club like Manchester City.

"The team sheet went up on a Friday and you looked at it and you were either in or not in. He never discussed why he was leaving you out of the team. It's no good me speculating on what he would've done if I went to him and asked his reasons why, I think Les McDowall gave you a fair crack of the whip. When you were playing well you'd be in the side. When you'd hit a poor run of form you'd be out. No-one knows better than the player himself whether he's had a good game or a bad game. It finished up there was more wing men on the books than any other position. I played on the left wing and I played on the right wing, but you also had Roy Clarke, Ray Sambrook, David Wagstaffe, Bill Spurdle, Harry Anders, of course Johnny Crossan came after me. They talk about having a big staff of players nowadays but when I played there we had every bit as big as squad as they have today. These days they call it squad rotation, back then you were just dropped!

"The thing was you see, I'd played for Hull City in the Second Division and I'd never come across Manchester. OK, I'd gone past it on my way from Dublin to Hull, but I knew nothing of the club. I knew there was a rivalry with United and they'd won things previously but that was about it."

Later on, Fagan moved to Derby County, having made his mark at Maine Road. By now, he was a regular for Ireland, he'd been voted Irish Player of the Year and turned in some fine performances for the boys in green when they played their football at Dalymount Park. This was long before the move to Lansdowne Road, home of the rugby side.

"Derby County... funnily enough the Baseball Ground was the worst pitch I'd ever played on. Maine

Road was bad then but Derby's was even worse! The manager at Derby at the time was Harry Storer, a blunt Yorkshireman. He couldn't do enough for me but I just couldn't settle down there so I came back to the North West.

"My son's godfather was a close friend of Peter Swales and Noel White and back in the early sixties, they had just taken control of Altrincham. So Swales was the chairman and a fellow called Cedric Boardman was the treasurer. They came down to Derby to see me because they knew I wasn't happy. They asked me to become player-manager of Altrincham, which I accepted, it suited me down to the ground."

Roman Abramovich has been making all the headlines by giving Chelsea all the money in the world to bring in a whole new squad of players. Although there is a big difference between Swales taking over at non-league Altrincham and a Russian oil billionaire taking over at Stamford Bridge, the Moss Lane outfit underwent something of a revolution under Fagan's management. He brought in a host of Football League players and immediately sparked an upturn in the club's fortunes.

"I played there and scored 12 goals in eight games but I got injured and I've never kicked a ball since. I had to resign after tearing ligaments in my knee, I just couldn't walk and had to wait to get it replaced, but not before I'd brought an influx of talent to the club. We really put the club on the map. Tommy Banks, the Bolton full back, Ernie Taylor, the former United and Blackpool inside-forward, they all came along and we had a great season."

These days Paddy is something of a regular on the City supporters network, visiting branches and attending sportsmans dinners here and there. The 50s era often gets overlooked when compared to the great teams of the 60s and 70s and Paddy helps to redress the balance. Youngsters who meet him are told of his deeds on that February day at Old Trafford.

"I get very well received at the supporters meetings I attend but I go because I try and give the supporters something back. I think the supporters want recognition because they're the ones that are backing you during your playing career. They love the club, so you've got to show your apreciaton to these people and I think they appreciate that back too.

"I'm always down at the ground and people will come up and say, 'Hello Paddy,' and I say, 'When's your next meeting?' I'm president of the City centre branch, there's Stefan and Maxine who run that branch - they're lovely people. I like going to places because I think they deserve it. Likewise, it's nice to be remembered because it's been a long time since I last played for City!"

PAUL LAKE
23RD SEPTEMBER 1989
FIRST DIVISION
CITY 5 MANCHESTER UNITED 1
ATT 43,246

"Five-One, we beat United Five-One", this was the City fans' chant not just for the rest of the season following the Maine Road Massacre of September 23rd 1989 but for many years after. In fact, the celebrations only really stopped when United took the title in 1993. While no major trophies came our way, those 90 minutes on that sunny autumn afternoon in South Manchester was all that a lot of City fans could celebrate during the grim 90s.

Later, the result was brought up by United fans in mockery of City's lack of success during the decade. Indeed, it wasn't until the brilliant one-two between Gary Neville and Shaun Goater in November 2002 that City recorded another derby victory during which time many supporters had almost given up hope of ever seeing another victorious derby day.

It's always worth remembering that before City's 3-1 win in 2002, City had won one league derby in 21 years. That's a hell of a lot of disappointments and pain to have to endure. Yet that sole derby win was indeed the famous 5-1 and looking back, whether it was an isolated result or not, whether the club didn't win any trophies for years afterwards or not, that game remains hugely significant in the history of the duels between Manchester's top two.

It is not a result that should be shoved under the carpet but one to be cherished, a performance to be recalled and savoured, a moment in City's history that should never be forgotten. And boy, did it hurt United at the time.

Chief architect of United's downfall that day was

Paul LAKE

Denton Blue Paul Lake, a City fan who fulfilled his dreams of playing for the club in the opening game of 1986-87 season, in a 3-1 win over newly-promoted Wimbledon.

His career was set for the highest levels possible before lady luck intervened when he picked up a cruciate ligament injury against Aston Villa in 1990. Two years of torture later, he pulled on the shirt again in City's first ever Premiership match, a 1-1 draw at home to QPR. He walked out to an emotional reception and when substitued after 70 minutes, the whole stadium rose to salute their hero, as they did when Lake was stretchered off in the 5-1 game. Two days later, on that awful night in Middlesbrough, not only his heart but those of Peter Reid, the other City players and the 3,000 City supporters present were broken when Lake collapsed in agony for the second time. His leg had gone again and although Peter Reid said at the time he would get the best treatment available to try and recover again, we all knew deep in our hearts that we'd probably seen the last of Lakey in a City shirt.

"When I look back at my career," says Paul, "alright it wasn't the longest of careers but there were some really important games in there. The first one was leading out City for the very first time as captain at Maine Road. That was against Everton and we won 1-0 thanks to an Adrian Heath goal. My first game as captain was against Spurs away, but the Everton game was special to me because we were playing at home."

The story of the young braves who started a whole new era for City: Lake, White, Brightwell, Hinchcliffe and Redmond has been discussed many times before and although White and Hinchcliffe went onto win full England caps, it was Lake who was thought of as the jewel in City's crown. Indeed many pundits at the time clearly believed he was potential England captain material.

Indeed, during City's 2 years in the Second Division following relegation, Lake played everywhere and anywhere, right across the back and midfield. 1987-88 was a huge learning curve for him and the rest of City's young team. Often they'd run up huge scores, often they'd concede nearly as many. Lake was also part of the famous 10-1 win over Huddersfield Town on November 10th 1987.

Yet Paul wasn't a prolific goalscorer but then again, he wasn't meant to be. One of his funniest moments was in the FA Cup at

ABOVE:
Paul Lake's
unquestioned
ability led to
him figuring
in Bobby
Robson's plans
before the 1990
World Cup
- only a lack of
experience saw
him omitted.

Blackpool where, after a truly abysmal performance, the sort that only City can produce, The Blues were spared an embarrassing defeat when they equalised in the last minute at Bloomfield Road. Both Lake and Paul Moulden claimed the goal after a goalmouth scramble, the announcer gave the goal to Moulden but Lake was halfway up the perimeter fencing shouting, "It was me! It was me!" at the City fans.

A far less happier moment was when he swallowed his tongue and nearly died on his beloved Maine Road pitch in the spring of 1988, when the visitors that day were Leicester City.

"I remember sprinting forward and making the run to the edge of the box and going up for the header and then... that was it really. I was out for the count. Next thing I can recall was when I came around, which was underneath one of the tunnels at the bottom of the stairs in the Main Stand. The first thing I saw were three women crying - my then girlfriend, my twin sister and another lady who was part of the medical team. They all thought I'd bought my ticket for the place upstairs, do you know what I mean!

"Geoff Durbin, who was involved behind the scenes at City even then, was one of my best friends at the club. I'd asked him to see a copy of the game as I knew he'd be filming all the games. He said to me 'Are you sure you want to see this Lakey, it's a bit gory', so I replied, 'Yeah, course I do, I want to see Trevor's [Morley] hat-trick don't I!' I will always be thankful to Roy Bailey and Dr Norman Luft for saving my life. Roy was over to me in seconds and I've got to say that Dr Luft is one of the loveliest blokes going, I met up again with him recently at the TNS game and we had a good natter."

Nevertheless, though the play-offs were just out of City's reach that season, the experience these youngsters picked up that season stood them in good stead for the following campaign. The sale of fans' favourite Paul Stewart meant a windfall for the club and a chance to bring in Brian Gayle and Andy Dibble, hero of Luton Town's Littlewoods Cup win over Arsenal. While the fans waited patiently for promotion to arrive, they sought their own entertainment, in the clubs, out on the streets and on the terraces on a Saturday afternoon. Manchester became Madchester. Rather than looking at City fans and thinking, 'God, they're going soft', the whole country followed the example of the Kippax lads as Lakey explains, "You know what I loved? When the blow-up banana craze started off, let's put it on the record that we started all that at City and that's something I'm proud of. After we did it, all the other clubs started carrying inflatables. It was probably a sign that half the crowd were off their heads or bored or simply just chillin' out but it improved the atmosphere at football matches all over the country. Stoke away on Boxing Day, we all ran out and threw bananas into the 13,000 City fans who were present that day out of a total of 24,000. It was like a home game, we still lost though - 3-1!

"Then there were the other ones: the paddling pool, the blow up doll, the egg, the Frankenstein and each one had its own little chant. I'd be taking a throw in or something and the crowd would be singing *"Paddling Pool, Paddling Pool, Paddling Pool!"* Our fans are innovative. They're trendsetters - they set the whole league off with that."

It's been said before that opposition managers used to instruct their teams to take the atmosphere out of the game at Maine Road. If it was 0-0 after 20 minutes the singing would die down a bit and if they nicked a goal, sometimes the home crowd would get restless with the City players. It's a theory that Lake has heard before.

"You do hear the crowd and certain comments and chants but being a player you develop a selective memory. You tend to block out certain chants and let others through. You noticed things when you played the home games. Not all the time but the Main Stand were often the first to start getting moody and having a bit of a moan, hence the phrase 'Main Stand Moaner'. Don't get me wrong, there were a lot of brilliant fans in that part of the ground, really supportive, but sometimes you could feel it on the side of the ground whereas the Kippax lads would try and counteract this and get the chants going. It's always been a bit see-saw at City and the Kippax did its bit at times to lighten the load and take the pressure off the players.

If we were losing or if some of us were having a mare of a game it was good to hear the silly songs and look over and see that lot entertaining themselves!

"Obviously, growing up in Manchester, we all knew what was happening out there but as a footballer you had to be disciplined. I feel we did miss out slightly on the 'Madchester' glory days but we all still went out on a Saturday night because you had nervous tension to get rid of, you had to let off some steam. If we were playing Saturday, we couldn't go out after Tuesday night and that was it. We certainly couldn't go out on a Friday night or anything like that but as a group we worked hard and we played hard.

"I used to be into all the indie stuff but also the dance music and I had two separate groups of friends for these things. I'd mooch out in places like the Haç, the Boardwalk, the Brickhouse, the Academy, the International, International 2... I used to go out on the razzle and enjoy myself but I couldn't go out every night like most young people in Manchester seemed to be doing at the time.

I used to love seeing good guitar bands, a lot of acoustic stuff, and I went to quite a few gigs in those days. I used to like Orange Juice, a good Scottish band, not to be confused with Orange Juice 'Dancing In The Rain' Jones! Then there was The Bible, Pearl Foundation, Aztec Camera. I went to a few festivals. Other times we'd end up in really cheesy places like Quaffers or Bredbury Hall - don't laugh - that's just the way it was in those days!

"On a Friday night you'd try to get some kip early because you needed to save your energies for the game so you'd get to bed early but often you couldn't sleep because you'd be thinking about the match. Then about 11 o'clock at night the phone would start going and it would be my mates. "Lakey, wa-hey we're in such and such nightclub, and we're all on the beer. It's rammed full of birds in here, you really should be here mate!" and I'd just tense up and fling the phone and just scream "Aaaaaarrgghh!!!!!!" Here's me trying to prepare myself for a big game on the Saturday and I've got these loons waking me up. Footballers have to be focused. It's no good trying to balance the two - you can't burn the candle at both ends."

City made a poor start to the 1989-90 season, Lake scored the only goal in a 4-1 home defeat by Oldham Athletic, a game in which former Blue Roger Palmer scored a hat-trick. The Blues soon clicked into gear and began rising up the table aided by the goals of fans' cult hero, Paul Moulden.

He's a player Lakey has fond memories of. "Paul 'Shoot' Moulden as we used to call him, was a fantastic talent but in the end maybe we all caught up with him a little bit. I remember playing against him when I was 12 for the City nursery side and we played against the Bolton equivalent. We lost 5-4 and Paul scored all 5 goals. You don't score 287 goals or whatever it was at that level and get into *The Guinness Book of Records* if you're a bad player. As a youngster he was very, very quick and he used to shoot from anywhere. To be fair, he was a cracking player and had nothing to prove to anyone but the simple truth was that Mel didn't fancy him in the starting XI as much as he did Trevor Morley. When he made the first team, he got found out just by half of one percent because he just needed a little more height and a little more pace just to keep him in possession of that shirt. Everyone else was as quick as him by then but having said that I still felt he had something to offer and should have had a run out in the top league when we'd got promotion.

"It's weird, different managers see players in different ways. Mel didn't fancy Moulden. Howard Kendall had just stepped off the plane from Athletic Bilbao and arranged for us all to go to the Isle of Man for a team bonding exercise. Ian Bishop was sat next to me on the plane and said, 'I'm leaving Lakey' and

I thought no way, he's winding me up, but it was true. You wouldn't think a star performer like Ian Bishop would be sacrificed in that way but that's just the way Kendall saw it.

"To be honest, I have a lot of respect for Howard and in his quieter moments he may sit back and think that he should have stayed at City and seen the job through. I think we'd have won things had he stayed on. The club was geared up for success, but the pull of Everton was impossible to resist. It's like if you were in a job and City came in for you - what would you do? I've worked at a number of clubs: Burnley, Oldham and now Macclesfield Town and I think it's brilliant here at Macc - I enjoy every single minute of it here. The only club though that's truly in my heart is City. One night Howard phoned me at home and said, 'I'm ringing to tell you I'm moving on, I'm going back to Goodison. I've loved it at City and I've fallen in love with the club but you don't get many second chances in life and that's why I've got to go back.'"

Of course, the Howard Kendall era came later in Lake's career. Before then though, there was the small matter of a promotion decider at Bradford to get through. A game Paul remembers well. "Bradford away. This guy ran on the pitch. [He had] long greasy hair, he's probably gone bald now or something but everyone still remembers him from this game. He legged it over to me and said, 'Look man, it's not happening. Palace are up four! Palace are up four! It's not happenin' man, it's not happening!'

"He had four fingers up to indicate the score from Selhurst Park but the way he spoke, he must have been drunk or stoned or quite possibly both because he was slurring his words

> "I used to be into all the indie stuff... I'd mooch out in places like The Haç, The Boardwalk, and The Brickhouse. I used to go out on the razzle and enjoy myself but I couldn't go out every night like most young people in Manchester seemed to be doing at the time."

and his eyes were all over the place. His words were coming out really, really slowly. I said to him, 'It will happen mate, it will happen' then he was escorted away by the stewards. One or two players came over to me and said 'what was he on about?' and I told them, 'he's trying to say Palace are 4-0 up', and they gave me a look back. No one needed to say anything, the look said it all. They took it on board straight away. We were playing well that day and I always felt the goal would come. We left it late but you can always rely on Tricky Trev to save the day, can't you! That supporter was doing his best to make a difference but I feel that we'd worked so hard and played so well that year that there was no way we were going to blow it all at Bradford... we left it late though!"

Morley's equaliser meant a 1-1 draw and a return to top-flight football. Lakey couldn't wait to show what he could do at the highest level having served his apprenticeship in the lower leagues.

"At the final whistle it was amazing with all the players being swamped by the supporters as they stormed the pitch. I missed out on the celebrations though. My then girlfriend had an engagement and she wanted me to attend so it was up to Blackpool with her. All the other lads went out in Manchester that night and said it was the best night of their lives - Manchester was a sea of blue - one or two of them, I understand, had to be literally carried home. The fans were buying them drinks all night and let's face it, you could have been Paul Lake, Nicolas Anelka or Geoff Lomax - if you were a Manchester City player that night the drinks were on the house! I had a couple of blues come up to me in Blackpool and buy me a drink but I missed out on all the jollies really."

So to 1989-90 where, in the first six league games, City started poorly, picking up a solitary win thanks to Clive Allen's snapshot against QPR. Then, the game before the derby saw a 2-1 defeat in the second round first leg at Brentford's Griffin Park. The derby match was on the horizon again and City were without the injured Andy Dibble, Neil McNab and Clive Allen. Things didn't bode well.

"Obviously, the fans were full of anticipation before the derby, they always are, but I couldn't sleep either and I was playing! We had Brentford in midweek and as a footballer you hear all the clichés and have to listen to all the advice that you are supposed to take each game as it comes but with me it was going in one ear and out the other. It was difficult to play at Brentford with the derby on the Saturday occupying most of your thoughts. It's hard to put it to the back of your mind. When you're a youngster it's hard sometimes to concentrate because you want the derby to come around straight away. I was often wishing my career away looking at the fixture list thinking, 'God, we've got a biggie in two weeks, United or Arsenal or Liverpool', so it was probably fair to say that we had one eye on the Saturday when we lost at Brentford in midweek.

"The 5-1 is my all-time favourite game really. As I said, we'd had a poor start and that's why we had to fight fire with fire. We were simply told not to be at all intimidated and to make sure they didn't humiliate us. Our only target for that game was not to be beaten. All week in the build-up there was banter everywhere you went and on my street in Denton there were a couple of United-supporting neighbours who were mouthy all week about what United were going to do on the Saturday. Afterwards, they were nowhere to be seen! The silence was golden!

"I woke up that morning and I was full of nervous tension. I just wanted to get it over and done with. I came down for breakfast and my dad exclaimed, "Cometh the hour, Cometh the Man!" I'll never forget that moment.

"The start was a million miles an hour and I think

the stoppage in play worked in our favour slightly. When we were back in the dressing room, there was nothing talked about tactics, we were getting updates about the fighting in the stands! When we re-appeared, we started better than them and we scored almost immediately. Dave scored a beauty from distance with a brilliant shot and obviously I've watched the video a number of times, but after that first goal you can see me clenching my fist and looking over to the bench. I thought, 'Yes, there's the first, now let's get stuck in and get some more. We've got the ascendency, now we can use the momentum. This is gonna be our day.'

"Getting the second almost immediately killed the game in my eyes. They were never going to recover from that. It meant we could settle down a bit and just play a slightly more patient game. When Bish scored the third, this just confirmed this in my eyes. Half time came and I didn't want to get off the pitch. We were hyper. Mel tried to calm us down. 'Remember Bournemouth,' he said, explaining that the game wasn't won and we'd have to keep it tight because it could happen again. We were told to make sure they didn't get any sort of foothold back in the game.

"So what happens? They score straight away and at 3-1 they had an eight or ten minute spell where they had us under the cosh. They almost scored again soon afterwards if I remember correctly. To be honest, that fourth goal was important. It gave us that breathing space once again. It took the sting out of any possible United comeback. They were gutted and then we hit them with the fifth. That goal, finished off by Hinchy, has got to be just the best team goal that's ever been scored. What a goal, that ball from Bishop to Whitey, who crossed it first time and Hinchcliffe's bullet header right into the back of the net. Where did he come from for that header?

"At 5-1 it was total ecstasy. 5-1 after 62 minutes

in the derby, you can't beat that. Given the years of hurt that followed and the lack of derby wins even, yes, it would have been nice to have done another Huddersfield, to have put seven, eight or even ten past them! To be honest though, we were absolutely spent. We'd put everything into that first hour, we really had nothing left and I think United were so down that they were happy to accept 5-1, accept their fate. They didn't want to concede any more, so the game sort of petered out. So yeah, it would have been nice, but you'd had settled for 5-1 before the game! Just a bit! In fact I'm buzzing now, I get goose pimples even talking about it!"

Ian Brightwell's never-to-be-forgotten wonder strike at Old Trafford meant a 1-1 draw in the return game. Howard Kendall had replaced Mel Machin as manager and picked up the reins of a relegation battle. After a goalless draw at Everton, City took maximum points from the holiday period, with a 1-0 win over Norwich and a 2-0 success over Millwall. The versatile Lake

LEFT: Lake's finest hour came in City's 5-1 demolition of United in September 1989, a victory celebrated here with Ian Bishop.

was employed at right back.

"I found it easy to play at right back because I had filled in there as youngster and in my school days. Having Whitey on the outside of me was an obvious advantage. We had a good understanding because he knew when I was going to knock it long or give a short pass. If he went to the wing I'd come inside a bit and if he went towards the box I'd create the overlap on the outside and things like that. Sometimes I'd knock it long over the full backs head for Whitey to race onto and of course no one was going to touch Whitey for pace, other times I'd push up and try and draw the full back to me and then play Whitey in along the ground. It's all about keeping the opposition full back on his toes.

"It's a bit like Peter Beagrie. He kept the full backs guessing by jinking and delaying his cross. Sometimes he'd delay it too long and the full back would get across and block and then at other times, when the full back thought he had Beagrie covered, they'd stand off him so he'd just cut inside and put it in the top corner from 20 yards! It's good to have a bit of arrogance about you when you go on the pitch - it gives your team-mates a little confidence boost when they see that in you.

"One game I was playing right back and I pushed up in the last minute and played Clive Allen in for the winner on Boxing Day against Norwich. It was a vital goal and I was ecstatic because Norwich were a good side with people like Andy Townsend and Robert Fleck. Howard was doing his nut at me, telling me to get straight back to the full back position!

> **"At 5-1 it was total ecstasy. 5-1 after 62 minutes in the derby, you can't beat that... yes, it would have been nice to have done another Huddersfield, to have put 7, 8 or even 10 past them! To be honest though, we were absolutely spent... and I think United were so down that they were happy to accept 5-1, accept their fate... but you'd have settled for 5-1 before the game! Just a bit!**

"We were a quick-footed, quick-thinking partnership and Dave used to drop back and defend as well. It wasn't the strongest side of his game but he had a go. He used his size to full effect and he got behind the ball and then it's up to the attacker to get past him. Show the player the corner flag, run him over there and do your best in those one-on-one situations."

City finished a respectable 14th in their first season back. 1990-91 saw the launch of one of City's best-ever kits, the all maroon one and with more quality signings in the shape of Tony Coton and with Niall Quinn settling in, the youngster from Denton was brimming with enthusiasm for the new campaign.

"The following pre-season we went to Norway and Howard pulled me to one side. He said he was going to play me at centre-half and he said he wanted me to make that position my own. Instead of me challenging Reddo and Big Col [Hendry] they'd have to fight me for the chance to play alongside me. Reddo had done nothing wrong and my heart went out to him but I had to change my mindset and take this opportunity. I think Howard just preferred me and Hendry as a partnership. I had already been something of a utility player now but I just wanted to hold down a regular position and stay there.

"The summer of 1990 was an exciting time for me. I was close to a full England call-up, I'd just missed out on The World Cup but I knew I had time on my side. I was really enjoying my football. During this trip Howard alluded that certain positions were up for grabs. Also there were three or four people in the running for the captaincy: myself, Reddo and Colin Hendry. I had a good game as captain in Norway when we won 1-0 against a local team. This sounds really sad but as this was my first-ever game as City captain I counted how many headers I won at the back during the game, I got up to about 23 before I lost count! At the end of that game, Peter Reid came over and said, 'just keep doing what you're doing and you'll be okay.' Peter was Howard's eyes and ears on the pitch so obviously that made me think why was he making a point of speaking to me, Reidy must have been party to any discussion involving Howard.

"So I knuckled down even more as I felt something was in the offing but on the eve of the Tottenham game I was walking around London just relaxing when Howard called to see me. Now I just thought, 'he's going to drop me! How could he drop me, after all the work I'd done?' Well I wasn't going to stand for it. I even had all my lines prepared and I was going to have a right go back at him. This is what I'd told myself about the situation. When he then asked me to be captain I couldn't believe it. I was as surprised as the next man! I think he'd left it to the last minute to keep the anticipation going or possibly to stop me getting nervous. Immediately, my thoughts went to Reddo whose place I knew I'd be taking."

The attraction of the two heroes from Italia '90: Gary Lineker and Paul Gascoigne together with a travelling support of 7,000 ensured White Hart Lane had a 36,000 full house for the start of the season. Lake, normally impeccable at the back, made an uncharacteristic error with a header and Lineker pounced to make it 1-0 in the second minute. City played well and were unfortunate to lose but the following Saturday saw the visit to Maine Road of Everton and a minute's silence for someone who needed no introduction to fans of either club - Joe Mercer OBE.

"As you know I've been a Blue all my life - a supporter, a player and it only struck me after I got home that night what I'd achieved. I sat in my chair at home thinking, 'flippin' 'eck mate, you've only just gone and captained City to a 1-0 win in the First Division'. I was so proud. My dad was in the crowd watching me and all my mates were in the stand too, egging me on. I looked over at the Kippax where I used to stand so many times and you know - things were going so well for me at that time. The next game of course was Villa, the game where the injury struck me down."

After getting the wrong advice and wrong sort of treatment in the early stages, Paul wasn't to know it but he wasn't to recover from his injury. Weeks of swimming, running, weights and knee exercises at Lilleshall were in vain. City, who were hovering around the top five for those two seasons, failed to take the next jump forward into Europe. The League was at times within City's grasp in 1992. What a difference to City's season a fully-fit Paul Lake would have made!

He was sent to America for an operation when he broke down again, however it was too late. His was to be possibly the last career-ending cruciate ligament injury. "Perhaps I had to go through what I went through for things to change. I was like the guinea pig, the test case, because now, players are getting the best possible tretament. Even if I had a player at Macclesfield Town, I'd still recommend they go and get the best treatment because that's what people deserve. You can't cut corners. Obviously, the things I went through - the mental and physical rehabilitation, mental and physical torture if you like, I was able to pass this knowledge onto long-term injury sufferers like Richard Edghill and Niall Quinn, although there were different consultants involved.

"It's very important to choose the right specialist, someone who you know is the best, wherever in the world that may be. You also need someone who has a very high success rate in

"As you know I've been a blue all my life - a supporter, a player and it only struck me after I got home that night what I'd achieved. I sat in my chair at home thinking, 'flippin' eck mate, you've only just gone and captained City to a 1-0 win in the First Division'"

these types of operations. Perhaps, because I wasn't a million-pound signing or star purchase, corners were cut. But if you're a trainee and come through the ranks and you're on peanuts and they probably know you'd play for City for nothing anyway then maybe it gave certain people an opportunity to find the cheapest possible option when in fact I deserved the best available treatment as well.

"After I quit the game, people think it was Roy Bailey who must've talked me into the physio role. I'd always had an interest in it because I knew a lot about it. I knew the various parts of the body and I'd had first hand experience of all these things. It was actually a lady called Mandy Johnson though, a beauty therapist who is now Manchester United's academy physio, who pressured me into doing it full time. She said, 'You've got half a brain, I think - use it!'

"So I help people, I can emphasise with people I can talk them through because I've been there. I went to Salford and did a study course and I got some help off the PFA and here I am at Macclesfield. Roy Bailey wrote me a lovely letter that I received soon after starting here, which was brilliant for me. It's gone from one extreme to the other now - the facilities at City are truly unbelievable these days. They really look after the staff.

"David Moss raves about his time at City and he feels it was a massive club even in his day. Him and Brian Horton didn't have a lot of money and I think looking back at all the managers I served, Howard Kendall is the nearest we had to Kevin Keegan now because he could attract the very best players and potentially the best players to the club. Reidy tried very hard to bring in a couple of players that might've made

> **"Perhaps, because I wasn't a million-pound signing or star purchase, corners were cut. But if you're a trainee and come through the ranks and you're on peanuts and they probably know you'd play for City for nothing anyway, then maybe it gave certain people an opportunity to find the cheapest possible option."**

the difference... but he couldn't get their signatures. Whereas Coton, Hendry, Reidy and Quinny were the spine of the team a few months after Howard arrived - in other words, he could get whoever he wanted and that's what a club like City needs. I think that team, which was just developing as I got injured, would do well in the Premiership these days. We had a good team in those days, but I'd like to think I was good enough to play in the current Premiership team too."

Paul Lake has long passed into City legend and he knows it. The amount of requests he gets for supporters' meetings, interviews and comments are astounding but it's something he's still more than happy to do. He's still approachable even with all the demands made on his time and he sees fans, directors, players, employees and everybody associated with the club as one big City family. "Jessie Ward, Roy Bailey, Stan Gibson. These were the faces you saw at Maine Road every day - it was like a family."

Paul was president of the Junior Blues and as far back as 1993 I was sat back in his office at Maine Road watching him sign card after card and reading through his fan mail - every single letter.

"I'm tremendously busy currently here at Macclesfield Town but I summarise now and again for GMR which I thoroughly enjoy and I do the odd little bit for stations like Talksport. I've also done little bits and bobs for the PFA. It's good to be still involved in football. The PFA and indeed the City fans helped me when I felt lost, it's always nice to give something back.

"It's nice to be held in such high esteem and I always go back to my testimonial. I was delighted with the turnout, over 22,000 which, especially as we'd had that long trip to Ipswich the day before and we weren't doing very well at the time. Then again, the City fans have always been absolutely brilliant with me and the ovation I received was out of this world.

Also, to put on the record, when I walked out I looked to my left at all the Reds and gave them a little wave. I was half expecting the finger, you know, 3,000 V-signs at me, but they sang my name and also gave me a brilliant ovation which really meant a lot to me - I'm very thankful for that. It was a great day for me and a proud day for all the family."

So there you have it - Paul Lake, a God in Manchester.

PAUL POWER
11ᵀᴴ MARCH 1981
FA CUP QUARTER-FINAL REPLAY
CITY 3 EVERTON 1
ATT: 52,532

For a lot of people, 1981 was a bad year. A very bad year indeed. Spiralling unemployment and crumbling infrastructure in many areas of society meant that it was one of the worst years ever for football hooliganism. It was also the year rioting erupted on the streets of Moss Side. Of course, City lost in the FA Cup Final but for Paul Power at least, one match in March of this troubled year provided him with one of his most treasured moments on a football field.

Paul was born in a year when City reached Wembley and, as we'll shortly rediscover, he did more than anyone to drive the Blues on to Centenary Cup Final success with a stunning five-goal salvo during City's gripping cup run.

An avid Blue, Paul has great memories as a fan. "I was a City supporter and I remember going to watch them against Schalke 04, a night match, the semi-final of the European Cup Winners' Cup. This was the Bell, Lee, Summerbee era of course, absolutely fantastic and I used to stand on the Kippax Street. Now that was one of the best City performances ever. When I first started going, I used to stand in the old scoreboard end and one of the first games I went to see was when Glyn Pardoe made his debut at the age of just 15. Dave Bacuzzi and George Hannah were in the team so it must've been mid-60s. I saw the Championship winning team but I didn't see all the games that season.

"Maine Road in those days was something special, because we were all together on the Kippax in one big group. Towards the end of Maine Road's time, I

125

felt the stadium had lost a lot of atmosphere and edge because it went all-seater. You had that bit to the right of the North Stand who were quite vociferous and lively and there was that other bit in Kippax Lower but they were split by the away supporters. That wasn't the case when I stood on the Kippax, we were all as one and there was nothing better than being all together - especially if we were winning."

Watching his boyhood heroes only whetted Paul's appetite and though he made his debut five years after Glyn Pardoe, when he arrived on the scene, he made his presence felt. Paul signed professional forms in July 1975 at the age of 20 because he was studying law at Leeds University. With the old team being dismantled and with injuries for much of the season to players such as Colin Bell, Tommy Booth, Dave Watson and Dennis Tueart, Tony Book blooded Power in the first team. Within a few games he had played a key role in the 4-0 win over Middlesbrough in the League Cup semi-final that helped City get to Wembley once more.

Power's rise continued the following season. He appeared against Juventus both home and away, was on the bench against AC Milan when the Rossoneri were defeated 3-0 at Maine Road before playing and scoring in the San Siro to secure City a 2-2 draw.

As Paul recalls, European football was a learning experience. "One other Euro game I remember was Widzew Lodz. We were 2-0 up at Maine Road and were pegged back to 2-2. Over there we drew 0-0 and went out on away goals. Joe Royle missed a golden opportunity in that tie and after that I don't think he ever pulled on a City shirt again.

"I also remember the Borussia Mönchengladbach game, which was the last in Europe until the TNS UEFA Cup-tie 24 years later. We drew 1-1 at Maine Road but we got beat 3-1 over there. They had Danish international Allan Simonsen and he pretty well ran the show from centre midfield.

"Allison had me at left back and I'll always remember that season we started the campaign with loads of experienced players such as Brian Kidd, Dave Watson, Kaziu Deyna, Mick Channon and Asa Hartford and of course that was the season that Mal came in half way through. So we had half of Tony Book's team against Mönchengladbach and on the pitch we had Tommy Caton, Nicky Reid and Tony Henry playing and I looked over to the dug-outs and sitting on the bench we had Kiddo, Dave Watson and Kaziu Deyna! It was too much for Nicky Reid and Tommy Caton that particular night, the movement of the Germans on their own pitch was too much. I think if Dave Watson had been playing from the start it might've been a different story."

The Germans went all the way in the UEFA Cup, beating Red Star Belgrade in the final. Had City picked the right team and progressed they might have gone the distance too, with only the Yugoslavs, MSV Duisburg and Eintracht Frankfurt left in the hat.

Anyone who lived through Allison's second spell at Maine Road will say, with hindsight, that Peter Swales pressed the panic button by bringing him back. One of the players who survived the cull was Paul Power.

"The game that I always remember was the League Cup semi-final against Liverpool. That was the team that Mal had left us because Bobby McDonald, Tommy Hutchinson and Gerry Gow were all ineligible for that competition. So we had players like Gary Buckley, Dave Bennett and then there were players like Nicky Reid, Ray Ranson, Tommy Caton, Steve McKenzie and myself. Players that Mal had left and we ended up getting to the semi-finals just because John Bond had come in, results had improved and the confidence about the place had improved and some of the players who couldn't get a result in the first part of the season were all of a sudden beating everyone.

"Now what happened in the first leg of the semi was absolutely scandalous. Kevin Reeves scored a great header, got in front of Ray Clemence and they've accepted it. Alan Kennedy and Phil Thompson are moaning at each other for not picking him up. The referee blew and we're all over at the linesman complaining but play was continuing and having been, or so we thought 1-0 up, we were nearly a goal down straight away.

"So we lost at home 1-0, Ray Kennedy scored but we drew 1-1 away, Dave Bennett hit the underside of the bar and it's like one of those Geoff Hurst moments but they were two really good performances. One thing to consider here was that in this era, late 70s and early 80s, we'd never had good results against Liverpool. I remember when Liverpool beat us at home about 4-0 and Kenny Dalglish turned Tommy Caton inside out and bent one past Joe Corrigan. So we'd never done well against that Liverpool side and come the semi-final we were all a bit apprehensive and we just thought we'd go out there and give it our best shot, which is what we did. I thought the referee's decision that night was diabolical, so nothing ever changes in that respect, does it!"

So this was the spring of 1981. John Bond had been in charge of City literally four months and not only was safety in the old First Division practically assured but The Citizens were eyeing a European return through a Wembley victory. No-one more so than Power, who seemed to be on a one-man mission to single-handedly bring the famous old trophy back to Manchester 14 for the first time in 12 years.

"We were lucky in the early rounds because we'd had two good home draws. We had Palace and Norwich and then we were drawn away to Peterborough and at that stage of the competition you'd settle for that. I think Tommy Booth scored that day and we won 1-0 at London Road."

In previous seasons, City had been humiliated by Shrewsbury Town and at Halifax, however the Blue Boys of 1981 were taking such tricky assignments in their stride.

"Then we got Everton away, that was the first bad draw we'd been given that year. I think Gerry Gow scored and I got the equaliser. Then you're thinking, 'if we can get a draw down there at Goodison then we could turn them over back at Maine Road'. We had good players in that team - Kevin Reeves was good at holding the ball up outside the box, Tommy Hutch gave us a little bit of width on the other side and with Gerry Gow and Steve McKenzie, you know, we had the artist and the workhorse, if you like. So we had a nice little mix going.

"At the back we had a couple of young central defenders in Tommy Caton and Nicky Reid and a bit of experience in Boothy to back them up. So, we'd been taking things a round at a time until then, but after the Everton draw you start to think, 'is it going to be our year?' We had the second bite of the cherry to come and we'd always fancy ourselves at Maine Road no matter who we were playing. We'd beaten Palace 4-0 and Norwich 6-0 so we didn't have a problem scoring goals."

More to the point, Paul Power didn't have a problem scoring goals! This cup run will always be remembered for the driving force and inspirational contribution of the City skipper. The third round tie had been billed as 'Bond versus Allison' and the former City Svengali received a hearty ovation from the Kippax faithful but as he left, the chants of "Allison, Allison" turned to "Johnny Bond's blue and white army." Two goals from Kevin Reeves, one a penalty, one from Phil Boyer and the other from Power himself completed the rout.

The 6-0 demolition of Bond's former club Norwich City on January 24th featured six different goalscorers. Again, one of these was Power. In the next round, Tommy Booth, by now a veteran of over 400 first team matches for City, guided the Blues past Peterborough.

So on Saturday March 7th, City took 13,000 fans to Goodison. It's a game Paul recalls fondly. "The equaliser I scored at Goodison was a great move. It was played up to Kevin Reeves who was as good as Kenny Dalglish at holding up the ball outside the box, although perhaps not as devilish inside the box, and I made a run past him, and he flicked it onto me. I lifted it over the keeper and made it 2-2. That goal was typical of how we played at that time. Build it through midfield and get up and support the forwards.

"John Bond was always of the belief that if you had good front men you'd have a good team. Phil Boyer was mobile and did superbly well for us at holding up the ball until he got a serious injury to his knee ligaments in round four. But he did the business for Bondy at Carrow Road and if you think back all the best teams, the most successful teams, they all had good front men who could win you the game. Leeds had Allan Clarke and Mick Jones, Liverpool had Keegan and Toshack and then later Dalglish and Rush. I've seen both sides of the argument, I've worked for Howard Kendall at Everton, who built his teams from the back and he always used to say if you're solid at the back and don't concede, you've always a chance of nicking it."

With City in such fine attacking form and with confidence surging through the roof, the scene was set for another glorious chapter in Maine Road's FA Cup history. 52,532 supporters packed into the famous old ground and the atmosphere was absolute bedlam as the countdown to kick off began. In those days the replay took place just four days after the original tie and the anticipation hung heavy in the air.

"That night provided one of the best atmospheres ever at Maine Road. It was simply electric. We could feel it warming up and in the dressing room we all looked round at each other, spurring each other on, looking for that win. We knew we could do it. The confidence had returned under Bondy, we were second bottom of the league after Mal had left and when Bondy came in we finished halfway up the league and of course we got to Wembley that year as well. It was probably those three signings in Gerry Gow, Tommy Hutch and Bobby Mac that gave us a little boost. They all had something in their game that we needed at the time.

ABOVE: Power jumps for joy having scored the equaliser at Goodison Park in 1981.

"Tommy brought a bit of craft, Gerry brought a bit of mettle and aggression and Bobby Mac just sorted out that left hand side, which also allowed me to play wider which felt more natural to me. Before that I'd been playing full back. Now we all know what went on off the pitch with Bobby - Jim Tolmie was another one - but it was allowed in those days and it didn't affect his ability to do it on the pitch and that's all that counted."

The facts speak for themselves. With a daring double raid on Coventry City to bring in Hutchison and McDonald and with a move to bring in the experienced Gow from Bristol City, The Blues had powered their way up the league, losing just one game out of ten between November 15th and January 17th. February's local derby saw the usual annual victory over the old enemy as a Steve McKenzie strike clinched a 1-0 win over United.

Even the presence of a Granada TV crew recording a now famous documentary on the fortunes of Manchester City couldn't shake the team's concentration.

"Actually, the head of the camera team was fantastic. He just said any time you want us in we'll film and anytime you want us out of the way, we'll just get out of the way. The cameras didn't bother me and it wouldn't have affected the senior pros but in all fairness, the younger lads, who it may have affected, were fine with the cameras too."

7.45pm and the teams ran out to a crescendo of noise and colour and City got off to a flying start thanks to full back McDonald. "He was different class, Bobby, at attacking corners. He would always pop up unnoticed. If somebody flicked it up at the near post, Bobby would be in at the far post, knocking it in because he judged the flight of the ball so well. Not the biggest but he had a good spring. He wasn't tall but he could get off the ground alright."

Power was attacking from the left side of midfield with Hutchison dictating the pace of the game on the right. Tueart and Reeves were making a nuisance of themselves up front. The screw was turning.

"When people ask me, 'What is the best goal you've scored?' I always say the one in the Everton replay. Villa Park in the semi was the most important but this one I remember as being the best. I used to get into loads of positions like that. I had a bit of pace and I'd get one-on-one with the keeper and I couldn't score to save my life, you know, but

Paul POWER

that particular night Dennis Tueart slid it through and I got away from the defence. I'm running with the ball, I just had the keeper to beat but I made my mind up early just what I was going to do. I just slipped it to the keeper's right-hand side, to my left and

it crept inside the post and everything just happened as I'd imagined, as I'd intended it. I felt composed when I was running up to the keeper and I remember the goal being a real striker's goal."

ABOVE AND OPPOSITE: Paul has been instrumental in developing City's Academy and the blue-shirted heroes of the future.

After the game an ecstatic John Bond faced the assembled press, "I think I believe in fairy stories. This certainly seems like one when we are only one step from Wembley after being at the wrong end of the division."

The fairy story continued for Power in the next round when his blistering free kick saw off the challenge of Bobby Robson's treble-chasing Ipswich Town. However, luck finally deserted the Sky Blues just eight minutes from time in the Wembley final when Tommy Hutchison deflected Glenn Hoddle's free kick past Joe Corrigan for an undeserved Spurs equaliser.

For all the despair of the replay and for the endless re-runs of Ricky Villa's amazing dribble, Paul Power's goal in the 3-1 win over Everton still remains a notable moment. It clinched City's place in the semi in front of the last-ever 50,000 plus crowd at Maine Road. Not even City's new home, the magnificent City of Manchester stadium, has the ability to pack them like that.

PAUL WALSH
FA PREMIER LEAGUE
CITY 5 TOTTENHAM HOTSPUR 2
22ND OCTOBER 1994
ATT 25,473

When radio commentator Brian Clarke came up with the nickname 'The Little Genius' for Paul Walsh he got it absolutely spot on. Walshie was an absolute gem of a player for City. Signed by Brian Horton in the mid-1990s when City were struggling at the wrong end of the Premiership table, his displays of passion and inventiveness endeared him to the City support. Yet one display stands out above the others. Walsh's finest hour for City came in a breathtaking 5-2 win over Tottenham Hotspur in 1994 - a game given double the time normally attributed to a fixture on BBC's *Match of The Day.*

At that time many top players were put off signing for City but Walshie had no qualms whatsover, "I was just so pleased to be back in the Premier League. There were a couple of other clubs in for me but I knew Brian Horton from earlier in my career, I knew his style of management and I knew how we would play. I also knew City, who were hovering above the relegation zone at the time, could potentially be a very big club again... however, I didn't realise just how much I would enjoy it up there. I mean, even now, I'd like to move back to Manchester and live there. I think it's a brilliant place to live.

"Of course Uwe signed round about the same time, the same week as myself, I think, so we only had one training session before Uwe and I played together on the Saturday. It was an awful game, we lost 1-0 at home to Wimbledon, and we followed that up with a 0-0 draw at home to Sheffield United. I was thinking, 'blimey, have I made the right move here or what?'

"Then Brian brought in Peter Beagrie, a winger who could get it into the box, someone who could cross it for me. Prior to that I was having to go searching for the ball, go outside the box and look for it, get involved in the build up play and then race back into the box and try and finish it off! Beag's arrival meant I could stay central and wait for the cross to come in.

"The first game we all played was at Oldham, which was another 0-0 draw but Beagrie hit the bar with a stunning free kick and I could see things happening. From there we went down to Ipswich where we put in a much-improved performance. They scored first but Beags took it down the left and I latched onto it as it came off the post. Then I slipped Uwe in for the second and although Vonky's diabolical challenge cost us a penalty, it ended 2-2 and we felt more comfortable with the system and Uwe and me were off the mark now. Obviously, it takes three or four games to develop that understanding and for everything to gel.

"From that night on the fans took to us in a really big way, which really helped. I'm not being cynical here but I think, when I signed for City, there was an element of 'why have we signed him? He's the wrong side of 30' from the City fans. I hated dropping down to that level to Division One and after 18 months at Portsmouth I thought here's a chance to play at the top level again for the next two or three years and I felt I played really, really well in my time at City.

"From there we beat Villa 3-0 on the Saturday where me, Uwe and Beags all scored together. Steffen Karl, remember him? He came in on loan and nicked the winner down at Southampton which gave us a bit of breathing space. We felt under a lot less pressure against Newcastle and came from behind to beat them 2-1. I scored some other goals that season - Chelsea in the 'Kippax Last Stand' game but once summer arrived me and Uwe looked at each other and felt we'd done a good job. We'd arrived, we'd turned it around and the fans were backing us. We felt good about the following season. Even now me and Uwe have that special relationship. I was shocked when he was diagnosed with chest cancer and we speak every couple of weeks on the phone. Some of the calls have been very emotional."

Niall Quinn had picked up a cruciate ligament injury in a home defeat against Sheffield Wednesday that season and had missed out on the Republic of Ireland's 1994 World Cup campaign. After making a marvellous recovery, he was banging on the first team door once again, eager to reclaim his place, but a partnership was already developing between Walsh and Rosler.

"The only difference between playing with Quinny instead of Uwe - the only downside if you can call it that, was that when Quinny was in the team it gave certain players the easy option of just knocking it long up to his head without any thought whatsoever. Up to his head every time, it was a lazy option which meant that one: our play was predictable and two: Niall had to do more work. When Uwe played, it meant we didn't have someone as powerful in the air, but nevertheless, he was quick thinking and sharp in the box.

"It meant we had to build up play more and find clever ways of playing the strikers in, so from that point of view, we played better football. Sometimes all three of us used to play. I think Niall Quinn was a fine player though. A good touch on him, no one in the league better than him at holding the ball up. We started that season pretty well. The West Ham and Everton games were a joy to play in. Then I scored at home to Palace and away at Sheffield Wednesday and in some other games before we got to the Tottenham 5-2."

With Walsh terrorising the opposition defences, the Blues were being feted as a great footballing side. Not just that but with two wingers, Walsh was scoring his fair share of headers!

The week before the Tottenham game, a Walsh-inspired Blues won 2-1 at QPR. City had been reduced to nine men following dismissals for Richard Edghill and Andy Dibble. It's a game Walsh remembers well, "Thousands of times I'd make that run at a back pass and try and put some pressure on the keeper, close down his angles. This time, Tony Roberts tried to clear but it hit me and looped over his head into the net. People may think it wasn't a very good goal or it was a lucky goal but I'm a striker and I can tell you that it's one I'm claiming because it was all down to my perseverance. In fact, it won us the game and put us eighth and I think that goal was a half-decent goal. It doesn't have to be a spectacular shot from outside the box, at the end of the day a goal is a goal."

So to Tottenham and this was a game where Niall Quinn (the big Irishman) partnered Paul Walsh (the little genius) instead of Uwe Rosler (the likeable German), with considerable amounts of ammo being fired in from Peter Beagrie (the artful dodger)! Confused? No wonder City fans forwent Brian Clarke's commentary on Piccadilly Radio and filled Maine Road to capacity.

The game had been talked up all week. Many thought it might be some sort of classic and that's how it turned out. Tottenham's line-up featured a galaxy of stars, many of them on duty in the World Cup the previous summer: England keeper Ian Walker was behind a defence that contained Sol Campbell, while Jurgen Klinssmann, Gica Popescu, Ille Dumitrescu, Teddy Sheringham and Nicky Barmby also featured that afternoon. Spurs' manager Ossie Ardiles favoured open, attacking football as did City boss Brian Horton.

City opened the scoring when Walsh pounced on a mistake in the box by Sol Campbell. Soon afterwards Klinsmann went tumbling down for the obligatory penalty which he duly dispatched past Dibble. Then in a devastating spell of action just before half time, City raced two goals clear. Walsh had his header parried by Walker following a Summerbee cross, unfortunately for Spurs it was parried straight into the path of Niall Quinn to score from close range. The third was a picture goal, a delightful shimmy on the halfway line from Beagrie who mesmerised two defenders with a cheeky step over before surging down the left. After leaving the hapless defenders for dead he laid the ball right into the path of Paul Walsh who stuck a boot out and diverted the ball over Walker at the Platt Lane end. This was also turning into one of Peter Beagrie's finest afternoons in a blue shirt.

"Beags was a great person to have round the dressing room. Okay, he can talk for England, but he's a real character, a very funny bloke indeed. On the pitch he was immensely talented, occasionally infuriating because he liked to tease his marker and hold onto it and try and beat the same player three times before crossing it... but he game me brilliant service at City."

Early in the second half, Spurs made it 3-2 and the City fans might have wondered if defensive frailties might come back to haunt them. They needn't have worried. The young midfield generals: Flitcroft and Lomas, who were keeping Steve McMahon out of the side, both found the net. Flitcroft's header capped a superb move that began with an astonishing Walsh dribble and ended with another pinpoint Beagrie cross.

The Sunday papers, Des Lynam and seemingly everyone in football lapped up this performance by Walsh and City. For a player who'd had his moments at Liverpool and Tottenham and apparently been consigned to the scrapheap of the First Division, it proved to be some comeback. Not only had Walshie proved that he had something to offer, but he was also now near the top of the goalscoring charts and in this swashbuckling new City outfit, he was the man who made the whole team tick. When he played, City played. As Paul says, "I said at the time I felt I had nothing to prove to Tottenham whatsoever, just to myself maybe."

Aided by the arrival on loan of Maurizio Gaudino, City went up to Newcastle and won 2-0 at a time when the Geordies were almost invincible on their own ground. Rosler scored the first after ten minutes and after 70 minutes of almost unbearable pressure, and after Andy Cole had missed about five open goals, Walsh added a second that saw the pair celebrate at the Leazes End in front of the delirious travelling contingent. However dreams of silverware were crushed in the next round following a spineless 4-0 defeat at Crystal Palace.

Around this time, City's form in the league took a real dip and from a position of relative security the Blues were being dragged into a relegation battle. The sound of the alarm bells around Maine Road was deafening. It was up to the same players that had dug City out of a crisis the previous season to repeat the trick, but in a season where four teams were to be relegated, one look at the Easter fixtures (Liverpool at home and Blackburn Rovers away) set nerves twitching.

Yet much to everyone's surprise, although it shouldn't have been that much of a surprise given the 'Typical City' factor that can rear its head at any part of the season, City beat the Merseysiders 2-1 - the winner coming from the head of Maurizio Gaudino. But there was still work to do as City went on to championship-chasing Blackburn Rovers. The Ewood Park outfit were the neutrals' favourites for the league and with rivals Manchester United drawing 0-0 at home to Chelsea earlier that afternoon, the City fans could cheer the side on knowing that an away win wouldn't necessarily be putting a nail in Blackburn's title coffin. After all, Premiership survival still had to be confirmed.

Walshie remembers the game with pride. "That was a hugely enjoyable game to play in. Kenny Dalglish commented to Sky TV after the game that City should be in the top six after producing the performance we did. Everyone was on top form in the team that night, I think we were spurred on by what we'd done on Good Friday against Liverpool. Liverpool had just won the League Cup the week previous so we went to Ewood Park with confidence and even when we went 1-0 down we were undeterred. We simply carried on and to be honest, we more than matched them that night."

In a game so dominated by City it was amazing that The Blues didn't take the lead until late in the second half when Walsh himself arrived at the far post to finish off Nicky Summerbee's goalbound effort. Alan Shearer and ex-City man Colin Hendry had scored for the hosts but a Keith Curle penalty, a Rosler sidefoot and Walsh's winner sealed the points for City in a match of high drama and skill.

To the watching millions on television and to the thousands of City supporters lucky enough to be inside the ground, the sight of the players hugging each other and Brian Horton bouncing around on the pitch, it looked like everyone at the club was pulling in the same direction. On limited resources, Brian Horton had kept The Blues in the Premier League for the second successive season. Yet for certain people that simply wasn't good enough.

"Much to the dismay of the players in the dressing room, the then chairman, who normally came in just to say a few words, seemed agitated that we'd actually gone out there and given such a great performance. We'd beaten Blackburn and there was a very strong possibility that our result made it that bit harder for him to justify sacking Brian Horton - which was certainly the vibe we got. The silence spoke volumes that night.

"Looking back we didn't win again after that and you begin to wonder about the politics at the club. Brian Horton was a good manager. He did the job at City with one hand tied behind his back. The way the chairman sacked him was farcical too, let's not forget that.

"Now if we consider that after weeks and weeks where no-one wanted to take the job, the writing was on the wall for the following season as a result of the horrendous mismanagement inflicted on the club at that time. The guy who Francis Lee eventually appointed after so long, his close friend Alan Ball, was the worst manager I'd played for in a long career. His decisions, his tactics, the way he addressed some of the players, were simply shocking. We were dead and buried before we'd kicked a ball that season. When he arrived at the club he gave a speech and it was tremendously inspiring and I thought things might be looking up again. I was wrong. I thought things were going to be upbeat but they were dismal.

"Let me also put something on the record here. What I'm saying about Alan Ball isn't meant to be personal in the slightest. When I was a young kid at Charlton I had a great game and Ball was the opposing manager, of Blackpool. Coming off the pitch he put his arm round me and said, 'Keep going son, you're going to be a tremendous player'. That meant an awful lot to me. I looked up to Alan Ball, respected him. Can you believe I even used to have a pair of his white boots!

"At the time, I never wanted to leave City but what annoyed me was a newspaper article linking me and Gerry Creaney in a swap deal. It was the first I'd heard. I went into his office and said, 'If you want me out of the club then fine but don't mess me about. I've worked hard here and I don't deserve to be messed about by someone like you!' I believe the City fans were upset when I left. To be fair to Portsmouth, they came back in with a three-year contract which gave me a lot of security at that stage in my career."

To this day Paul Walsh remains a firm favourite with the City supporters who speak to him on his stints on *You're On Sky Sports*, ITV's *The Goal Rush* and Eurosport. "To be honest," he comments modestly, "my main line of business is property development but it's good to keep your hand in with a bit of TV work. I really enjoy it. These days I watch City's progress from a distance and after that first season back you've got to say City are a team in that middle section of the Premiership looking to make that jump into the top section - a jump that is awfully difficult to do. If one team can do it, though, it is City, they have the fan base, they have done well in the transfer market and the manager will keep pushing them on. I'm sure Kevin Keegan was slightly embarrassed that they qualified for

"The guy who Francis Lee eventually appointed after so long, his close friend Alan Ball, was the worst manager I'd played for in a long career. His decisions, his tactics, the way he addressed some of the players, were simply shocking. We were dead and buried before we'd kicked a ball that season."

Europe through the fair play league but they have to grasp such an opportunity with both hands because the profile of the club increases when you're involved in Europe. From now on European qualification has to be the target every year, qualifying through league position. For those brilliant fans though it must be great. Soon they could be packing their suitcases for AC Milan. When I was there they were going to the Isle of Man!"

PETER BARNES
12ᵀᴴ NOVEMBER 1975
LEAGUE CUP FOURTH ROUND
CITY 4 MANCHESTER UNITED 0
ATT: 50,912

Peter Barnes is one of those rare people who has pulled on both the sky blue of Manchester City and the red of Manchester United. He wasn't at Old Trafford for long and it's quite obvious that his heart is 100% with City. It is no surprise either to learn that Peter's fondest memories are of playing for City in the Manchester derbies. Although he scored at Wembley in the League Cup Final against Newcastle United, it was the fourth round triumph over Tommy Docherty's United that set the Blue boys on their way to the Twin Towers.

This was a game that left the United support traumatised and humiliated. They kept their heads down in work, school and pubs for sometime to follow. At the time though, no one in the blue corner realised how bad the injury to Colin Bell received actually was. It proved to be the beginning of the end for his magnificent career.

While 'King' Colin was facing the final curtain, a fresh-faced Peter Barnes was very much at the beginning of his glittering career. It wasn't Peter's derby debut but it was his first victory at Maine Road in a derby encounter. It was also the first time he'd enjoyed the cheers of the Kippax faithful as he raced down that left hand side at Jimmy Nicholl and the rest of the United back line.

"United had just come back up again from the Second Division, but even then had been amazing because with United down you'd imagine the derby match would've been off the agenda for a least a year. But we drew them in the League Cup at Old Trafford and went down 1-0. So the battle over supremacy had continued while the clubs were in separate divisions. So when the draw came out again, the city of Manchester went absolutely mad. It also gave us players the chance to redress the balance and re-assert our authority in these matches.

"The thing about the derbies is, you want to win the game for the fans. The supporters are coming up to you for a couple of weeks before the game telling you how important victory is. I was brought up in Manchester and I knew all about it. It makes me laugh when United fans say the game they look forward to most is Liverpool. Okay, I understand they are two fine clubs who have won many European Cups between them, but if you're from Manchester, the only game you really want to win is the City v United game. It's everything."

Certainly Peter Barnes would have been steeped in the culture of Manchester derbies by the time this fourth round League Cup tie came around. No doubt he had been regaled with the tales of City's glorious past by his father, the great Ken Barnes.

"We'd lost that game 1-0 as I say the previous season and what I remember about that night was all the Stretford End was be packed full of United fans and the Scoreboard End was packed full of City fans. The other thing that set the derby match aside from the others was you knew the opposition would have a lot of tickets for their support. The atmosphere was deafening, as it was at Maine Road the following year. Like I say, we wanted to win the derbies, not only for the fans but also for ourselves. These are the games you want to play in and win. Looking back at that time, both sides had some great players. I was in the team but I knew I was there on merit and that was a great feeling. I still had butterflies before this one though, because it was such a big game for us.

"I used to get superb service from Asa and Willie

OPPOSITE:
A typical
winger,
Barnes' style
and swagger
was an
important
dimension in
City's success
in the 70s.

on the left. There was Colin in the middle, Dennis Tueart and Big Joe Royle up front. Big Joe in net, Mike Doyle, Alan Oakes, Glyn Pardoe - people who'd done everything in the game. Joe Corrigan I'm sure gave me a few words of advice before this game, I'm sure his words were, 'Just go out and express yourself. Go and enjoy the game. Get at the full backs and create things for the strikers.' Hearing that was fantastic, it gave me a boost knowing the players around you have confidence in you and faith in your ability.

"United also had Stevie Coppell, a great winger who would cut inside and Gordon Hill on the other side. I felt I had slightly more in common with Gordon, mainly because he played on the left and he was an out-and-out winger. I feel the game today lacks pacy wingers. What can be better than taking it all the way to the goal line and swinging the ball straight into the box? Both were good attacking sides and the players City had at the back and in midfield meant I could do my job without hindrance, which was to get the ball and provide the service for our great front men.

"We ran out and the noise was absolutely incredible. Dennis scored an early goal for us that gave us the platform to get the ball down and play some great football. We gave a great exhibition and played the game as it should be played in my opinion.

"United had some tough players: Gordon McQueen, Joe Jordan, Jim Holton, and Martin Buchan. Obviously it was Martin who clashed with Colin Bell. Colin used to provide me with crossfield 50-yard balls from the right straight to my feet. As I said, most of my service came down the left but Colin's vision was incredible and sometimes he'd pick me out with a diagonal ball. It's hard to describe exactly how good it was to play with Colin Bell. Only those who have experienced it know what I mean.

"Colin went off and we didn't realise just how bad things were until about ten days later. We came off the pitch ecstatic because of that superb performance, everything had just clicked into place on the night. We thought Belly's injury would be a few weeks. When he came back from the specialist and it was diagnosed as knee ligament trouble, we were absolutely devastated. I spent some time on the injury table myself the following year and I saw first hand what Colin had to endure, the mental and physical torture, just to get himself fit once again."

These days Peter runs a successful business called 'Kik-Off'. After a stint involved with junior football, Peter believes there weren't enough playing areas for children so he decided to do something about it.

"I feel very passionately about the game, especially at grass roots level. The kids need a safe place to play and when they do have one, they should be encouraged simply to enjoy the game and improve their skills. So we're in partnership with a number of people and we provide Astroturf pitches so that, across the Greater Manchester area, where there so many good players waiting to be spotted and developed, the next generation can have somewhere to play. I like to see the kids playing football rather than sitting behind a computer screen or watching TV and videos. So if I can give something back to the game that's done so much for me, then I'm delighted."

RODNEY MARSH
27ᵀᴴ SEPTEMBER 1972
EUROPEAN CUP WINNERS' CUP
1ST ROUND 2ND LEG
VALENCIA 2 CITY 1
ATT: 35,700

These days you open the papers and it's Marsh. You turn on the telly and it's Marsh. Switch on the radio and they're talking about Marsh again. Marsh this and Marsh that! Is there any escape from that blasted Marsh character? That's enough about Jodie though! Back in the seventies everyone talked about another Marsh, Rodney Marsh. Of course Rodders is still a highly prominent figure in the football world, being a regular pundit on Sky TV where his performances on *Soccer Saturday* and *You're On Sky Sports* often get talked about as much as the actual games he is reporting on.

Back in 2001 I spent a whole day behind the scenes at Sky TV watching *Soccer AM* being filmed from the sidelines, followed by the full six hours of *Soccer Saturday*. That was the first time I'd met Rodney. I felt a little bit in awe of him, which was probably a bit silly really, but I knew he was a legend and even then he had an air about him, a presence, a confidence about him that everything he would touch would turn to gold.

He's not right about everything of course. He famously made those remarks about Bradford being relegated and of course they stayed in the Premiership which meant he had to have his hair shaved off for charity. His forthright views have often come back to haunt him, but at least he is great entertainment. Readers who remember his playing career may see a link developing.

When I ask him about the success of *Soccer Saturday,*

Rodney just says, "We tell the truth. If someone misses a sitter, two yards in front of goal, you don't say, oh he was unlucky or it bobbled a bit on the grass. You just say what the fans would say - that was rubbish! Why should we water down our views when we really want to say something else?"

Rodney Marsh is an original. He can't be anyone else and, to be fair, doesn't try to be. There are arguments that say this highly talented player should have achieved more. Yet he did win eight of his nine England caps while at Maine Road and he provided the City support with some moments of real quality. For someone who was supposedly the 'wrong signing' for the club, he made an awful lot of people happy.

"I have many, many memories of my time at Manchester City but one game I hold dear to my heart was the trip to Valencia in the UEFA Cup. We'd drawn 2-2 in the first leg at Maine Road and I scored on that night, together with Ian Mellor. Of course that meant the Spaniards had two away goals and it would take an incredible performance to get a win over there. They were just as good then as they are now. Di Stefano was their manager at the time, one of the greatest players of all time without any shadow of a doubt.

"I scored in the second leg too, in the sweltering heat of Southern Spain. It was a brilliant goal, which, because there were very few travelling supporters and probably no TV coverage of the tie, no one has really seen. Mike Summerbee took a corner, it was flicked on by Tommy Booth and I scored with a belting overhead kick. They were two exceptionally good games of football to have taken part in. Like I say, the tie meant a lot to me as it was my only trip with City into Europe during my time there.

"My first derby experience was at Old Trafford. We won 3-1 and I scored on that day too. To have played in that atmosphere, having heard so much about it, was something else. I had no qualms about moving North. Okay, I was a London boy, but just because I was on new territory I felt that if something needed to be said, then I'd say it. Just because I was moving to Manchester that wasn't going to stop me. It got me into a lot of trouble but that's just the way I am.

"Towards the end of the 1971-72 season we played some great games against Derby, the champions, for example. We got to Wembley but I've gone on record before as saying I didn't want my losers medal, it was something I just didn't want to keep in my possession. Then there was a game in early 1975 when we beat Middlesbrough 4-0. I remember lots of important games during my time at City."

Rodney's overall record was one goal in every three games during his City career. Not prolific by any stretch of the imagination, but he was a central figure in a soap opera that involved managerial disputes, boardroom battles and a transitional period on the park as well. During a time of chaos, Rodney's skills warmed the hearts of the City faithful. Although, as he knows, he wasn't everybody's cup of tea. A straight talking man deserves a straight talking question. How does he feel about being labelled 'the man who cost City the 1972 championship'?

"Well I've had this rammed down my throat wherever I've gone in the last thirty years and although I've kept a dignified silence about this but I actually welcome the chance to say something about this to the City supporters. I know a lot of that team, Francis Lee, Mike Summerbee, Mike Doyle, and two or three others have all had their say on this - although, I might

"Well I've had this rammed down my throat wherever I've gone in the last thirty years... Francis Lee, Mike Summerbee, Mike Doyle and two or three others have all had their say on this - although, I might add, that none of them have ever had the decency to say it to my face. I actually agree with them - that if City hadn't signed me, they would've gone on to win the league"

150

add, that none of them have ever had the decency to say it to my face. I actually agree with them - that if City hadn't signed me, they would've gone on to win the league, but I'm not the manager. The manager buys the players and if they want to sign me from QPR for £200,000 then that's their decision. What I disagree with and, to be quite frank, what I resent is this trial by players that I've had to put up with."

Rodney mentioned di Stefano and of course, the famous Argentinean was the player Santiago Bernabeu built his Real Madrid empire around. Perhaps the success of a star striker is down to others in the team changing the style to suit him. "City knew what my game was when they signed me. I actually agree that my game perhaps wasn't best suited to the way the team played normally but if they are going to bring me in as the new striker, they should've played to my strengths. Rather than me trying to change my style to accomodate them, there's an argument that says they should've changed to accomodate me.

"Any striker needs six games or so to bed in but I was thrown straight in at a critical time of the season. Perhaps, if they'd have trained me up and kept me on the bench till the new season, then City would've won that League, I would have started the season with a clear name and everyone would have lived happily ever after. For example, if Newcastle buy Alan Shearer, then he would want them to give him the service he wants, he would expect them to change their style of play to suit him. There are things professionals might say in private but I feel it's wrong to keep making me the fall guy thirty years on."

Rodney obviously isn't on everybody's Christmas card list. However was there any bad feeling back then? Was there a clique against him at Maine Road?

"No, not really. I didn't feel there was a clique against me. I had good friends in the dressing room, after all they made me captain of the club, which was something that made me feel immensely proud."

For all the debates and personal comments that have clouded this chapter in City's chequered history, at least the relationship between Marsh and the fans has remained unscathed. It is something Rodney truly appreciates. "I've gone on record many times before in interviews and on the TV and said I firmly believe that City have the best set of fans in the country. I always say what I feel honestly and I think it's definitely true. They're fanatical about their team. They always lifted me, the City crowd, they were always on my side and it was them who gave me the confidence to go and try the things I did. I loved it up there at City, it was truly great."

By the end of the 1973-74 season Tony Book had picked up the pieces following the Mercer-Allison split and the Ron Saunders fiasco and City boasted a forward line of Bell, Lee, Summerbee, Marsh and Law. The names rolled off the tongue. As mentioned previously, the nearest City got to success that year was the League Cup Final defeat against Wolves in 1974. However April 27th of that season provided Marsh with one of his most satisfying moments.

"I was actually injured that day, when we sent United down. To experience that was incredible, you had to be there to understand what I mean, but I was so pleased for our supporters because I was so pro-Man City and so anti-Man United. Denis was devastated, he truly was. When he scored I said to Tony Book, 'Get him off now,' and I can recall him trudging off the field before the fans swarmed on trying to get the game called off. I haven't lived up in Manchester since the 70s but I know how incredible it is up there with the rivalry."

Within a few seasons City were topping the First Division again and, although they dropped away, the seeds of success were being sown. Yet Marsh wasn't happy with the way things were going and looked to get things changed. "I just felt we were going backwards under Tony Book. So first of all, I grabbed a word with the coach, Ian McFarlane but he wouldn't take my views on board. Then I sought a meeting with Tony Book and after he wouldn't listen I went straight to the top and spoke with Peter Swales. The team was disintegrating. Summerbee and Lee had been sold on, obviously later on Colin Bell's injury was a devastating blow. I knew the writing was on the wall when we brought in Barney Daniels as striker! That's no disrespect to him as he's a smashing lad but he wasn't the sort of player we required at the time.

"I was the captain and I felt I had a role to play. I'll give you a little anecdote. I never tire of telling this story. The beginning of the end was when we played a League Cup tie at Norwich and with a quarter of an hour to go, we were losing 1-0. I waved Mike Doyle forward and said, 'Go on Doyley, get up the field we'll play with three at the back. We need an equaliser here.'

"Then I caught sight of the bench where Booky and McFarlane were in absolute uproar! They were screaming at me, 'Whizz, whizz, what are you doing? Get him back!' (my nickname was Whizz at the time) so in the end I said, 'You'd better go back Mike, they're doing their nut!'

"Five minutes later, we were still losing and I thought 'sod this'. 'Mike', I said, 'Get yourself forward

BELOW: 'Me and my big...' Marsh in action against United in 1976.

153

again and stay up there,' and within a minute he'd got the ball in the box and whacked it home for 1-1. My decision had helped bring about the goal. I think in the replay we won by six goals to one but if we hadn't pushed Doyley up front we would've been out of the Cup and the management team knew it. Afterwards they didn't speak to me. They never said 'well done' or anything like that. Like I said, perhaps a captain doesn't have those responsibilities but I felt it was the right thing to do at the time."

These days Rodney sees a lot of City, which means he can't use his usual line of complaint, 'They've given me the worst match again!' Would he have enjoyed playing in Keegan's free-flowing attack-minded outfit?

"I think the way Kevin Keegan sends his sides out is absolutely fantastic, you know. It's a breath of fresh air for the Premiership. Some people set their stall out not to concede whilst others look for the win all the time. That's opening up a whole other debate about football but I've never been one of these people who says he's tactically naive or anything like that. He knows what he's doing but he still thinks like a striker and you can see that in his team's formation. Everything is geared to getting that end product - a goal. Obviously when the other team is attacking the emphasis has got to be on defending, but City now are always looking to find a goal, they're not the sort of team to sit back or anything.

"The greatest player of all time was Pele and he said that you only really have five great games a season. The rest of the time you could win but you don't play that well. However when you fill your forward line with any number of players who can win the game for

"I was actually injured that day, when we sent United down.
To experience that was incredible, you had to be there to understand what I mean, but I was so pleased for our supporters because I was so pro-Man City and so anti-Man United."

you, you're eventually going to open them up and get something because at least one of them will be on form. City on their day can be a magnificent team to watch. I love the club and I love the fans and I look out for their results all the time."

ROY LITTLE
MAY 11TH 1956
FA CUP FINAL
BIRMINGHAM CITY 1 CITY 3
ATT: 100,000

Talking to a gentleman like Roy Little is truly an invigorating experience. His post-war career spanned nine glorious years, in an era when loyalty to the club and pride in wearing the shirt meant far more than picking up a win bonus. A different era, a different mentality yet a heart-warming tale nevertheless about one of Manchester City's true unsung heroes. Roy was born in Miles Platting, an area that has remained underdeveloped until the City of Manchester Stadium breathed new life into the surrounding districts. Before the war the family moved south to Wythenshawe, as many Mancunians did, to a lush green area of land which later expanded into the biggest concentrated housing estate in Western Europe.

It was while Roy was growing up in the Northern Moor area that he discovered his passion for sport. Although, as Roy explains, if fate had not intervened at an early age, he may have been making his name playing the fifteen-a-side game. "I attended Manchester High on Whitworth Street, which was a very good school indeed. However we must have been seen as somewhat snooty because we weren't allowed to enter a team in the Manchester schools football competitions. Now this rule only applied to ourselves, Manchester Grammar, Chorlton High and Burnage High, and for the life of me, I don't know why!

"I used to absolutely adore school sports days and the sports classes we'd have during the week. The school mainly concentrated on rugby and hockey. Now, one day when I was about 12 I was playing at hooker in a rugby match and there I was feeding the scrum when I took an almighty whack in the face. So that was me, out for the count. It was like one of those cartoons, I was seeing stars in front of my face! So they told me to leave rugby for a bit and start playing football, which was considered to be a less dangerous game! By the age of 13 I was in the school XI, playing with lads much older than myself, which only improved my ability all round. I knew I was good for my age though.

"People were aware of my ability and word was beginning to spread. On Saturday mornings I'd play for a team called 'Rackhouse' in the under-18 Wythenshawe League. Again, I was only 13 or 14, fitting in with boys much older than me but it was giving me such great experience. But it was illegal what I was doing and I had to tell me dad I'd tripped over some barbed wire on my way to watching them when in fact I'd been tackled during a game! In fact, I've still got the scars on my leg which were from those very early days!

"Then I played, legally, for another Wythenshawe League team called Greenwood Victoria. We entered and won a competition called the Christie Cup, named after the hospital in Withington and this put me firmly in the spotlight. A few people had come down to the final and a bloke who introduced himself as a City scout offered me and a friend a trial down at Wilbraham Road. We naturally thought there would

only be a handful of players there but when we got there, there must've been at least 200 players, all under the guidance of City coach and former Everton player, Charlie Gee.

"It was there at that training session that I was put at full-back. Previous to that I'd always been a left winger, because I was right quick in those days. I never used to mark anyone, I always got a game because I was left-footed but here I was being asked to stay back and mark up. Well, it wasn't what I'd expected but by now I was desperate to play for Manchester City."

Roy had been quite a prolific goalscorer in junior football but during his City career he would only score twice for the Blues. However, he was not to know that when he signed amateur forms for Jock Thompson.

"In those days of course there was conscription and I was sent to the RAF base in Shropshire. Jock Thompson was very shrewd and gave me a professional form to sign. It made me a part-time professional, I'd play in the 'A' and 'B' teams, the reserves etc and if anybody was to try and sign me they'd have to go through Jock first, as he had the contract. I received a £10 signing on fee and my wages were £6.50 a week, with £1 extra for a draw and £2 for a win! Everybody in football got virtually the same money in those days.

"I'd had some experience with the Under-18s at Maine Road before spending two years in the forces. I played for the RAF first XI and in Shropshire I was told to go to Wolves because they'd seen me and wanted me to attend a trial. Then I was posted to the RAF base in Kirkham, Lancashire and was told to report to Preston North End, who gave me a few games in the reserves but they couldn't poach me, because Jock Thompson had already covered himself.

"Then Thompson had been replaced by Les McDowall and I had six months still to see out in the forces. My heart was set on City but I knew there were probably four or five full backs waiting to get into my job and that a new manager may have his own favourites. I also knew that they weren't any better than me and nobody could beat me for having pride in that blue shirt. I had accepted that I'd have to work hard to impress a new manager and I'd have to force my way into the reckoning, but after a long spell in the reserves I eventually got my chance, making my debut in the 1951 FA Cup tie against Swindon Town at Maine Road."

City won the game 5-1. Roy was now a first team player and his love affair with The FA Cup had begun in earnest.

"The Cup final WAS the be all and end all. The FA Cup is supposed to be THE trophy of the football world and to take part in that is tremendous. The first time you walk out at Wembley it's awesome - absolutely awesome. The crowd are 30 or 40 yards away and there were 100,000 people there although you might possibly have squeezed a further 20,000 in. The place wasn't even covered then but for some reason, I don't know why, the weather was always boiling hot for Cup Final day!"

1952-53 saw Little slowly improve although City's form generally could only be described as indifferent. Little blamed the inconsistency of the performances on the inconsistencies of the manager. "Every player is allowed to have the odd bad game but it would seem that Les McDowall didn't have the patience to find out what was wrong with certain players. He'd just drop you! No explanation, but as I say, I'd always feel that I would, in time, regain my place because I was the best left back at the club at the time."

Just as in the 60s and 70s when Joe Mercer used to go and play golf 2 or 3 days a week and leave Allison to take the coaching, so McDowall often left the team in the capable hands of Lawrie Barnett.

"To tell you the truth, he was a very quiet sort of

ABOVE:
Roy Little in
his salad days
- a time when
City were
undisputed
Cup Kings

manager. We didn't see him a great deal, he wasn't one of those tracksuit managers that you see nowadays, Les would never take his collar and tie off. You knew he was up there in his office and you'd see him occasionally but he still must've known what was going on round the club. He used to put the team sheet up on a Friday morning when we were out training and then buzz off home immediately! If we'd been dropped, we couldn't say anything about it anyway, because he wouldn't be there!"

Something had to change. Luckily enough though, something was about to change. Enter a new striker called Don Revie and the 'Revie Plan'. McDowall, for all his quietness, was tactically aware and his hard working players were using reserve team games to trial the idea of having one deep-lying centre-forward, supported by two forward attacking players. It was Johnny Williamson, not Don Revie, to whom the plan owes much of its success. Once Williamson, Revie's centre forward understudy, had mastered the technicalities of the plan in the reserves, the mantle passed to Don and the first team players to adapt for real.

Whereas previously McDowall's boys had been simply re-establishing themselves in the top flight they were now looking forward to games with renewed confidence. Teams didn't know how to play against City as the Blues made it to the top four in the league and, more notably, to two successive FA Cup Finals at Wembley.

Of course, back in the thirties, City went to Wembley in 1933 where, in the first final to feature players with numbers on their backs, the Blues went down 3-0 to Everton. At the end of the game, Sam Cowan, the City captain, told King George V that City would return victorious twelve months later, which they actually did, beating Portsmouth 2-1.

After the final whistle, neither Roy Little, nor captain fantastic Roy Paul had such thoughts of doing a 'Sammy Cowan'. "To be honest," muses Roy, "the second cup run just seemed to happen really. We took it game by game and of course, we were given this fantastic opportunity 12 months down the line to set the record straight."

The 1954-55 season had seen City defeat United three times that season, including a 5-0 thumping at Old Trafford and a 2-0 win at Maine Road in the fourth round of the Cup. Prior to that game Matt Busby had said that the winner would probably go all the way in the competition. So it almost proved, with the Blues overcoming Sunderland in the semifinal in 1955. Their opponents were north-east rivals Newcastle. "No disrespect to York," says Little, "but we wanted to play Newcastle because we wanted a really big draw for the final. York might have been easier, but then again, with fate as it is, we might not have got back the following year."

The story of the 1955 FA Cup Final has been well documented elsewhere but for a long time it remained Roy Little's personal nemesis. "I'm so glad Di Matteo scored that early goal for Chelsea a few years ago against Middlesbrough because Jackie Milburn had held the record for the earliest Cup Final goal for so long... and it was me that missed the bloody ball! It went over my head into the net, so yeah, I'm delighted that record has gone now. Newcastle seemed to settle down before us and before you knew it, we were chasing the game.

"You see, in those days, in the Cup Final, there was usually an early goal scored but never that early! There had been a bit of frustration amongst the City players though, which didn't help matters. We were the first club to wear tracksuits and it was about 84°F that day. We're all boiling hot because we were warming up in these tracksuits and when they told us to start the game, we were a little late because we couldn't get the bloody tracksuits off!

"There were no substitutes in those days, so Jimmy Meadows' injury was a critical moment. It was bad enough at the time because only 17 minutes had elapsed and if you remember, we were playing the Revie Plan and we didn't legislate for things like that. So we started with four forwards and Bill Spurdle was on the right and Billy came back then which only left us with three forwards. Poor old Jimmy turned to get at Mitchell, their good winger, but I honestly believe that on the day, even if we'd had eleven players, we would still have been beaten by the odd goal."

So there was no declaration of intent from Roy Paul about returning the following year, but return they did, in 1956, against Birmingham City.

"We were very fortunate to go back the second time. That's when you actually savour the atmosphere because you know what it's like. That helped us in the second game. The atmosphere was probably the same as in '55 but our thinking was different. It was easier relating to that Wembley turf second time around. Funnily enough, I've got the video of the 1956 game and they've all got cloth caps and rattles. There's the man with the white suit and everybody waving their songsheets!

"In 1956 we had no fear. We got stuck in and we all did our particular jobs. I never used to go beyond the half way line - my job was to pick up their No

> "In 1956 we had no fear. We got stuck in and we all did our particular jobs. I never used to go beyond the half way line - my job was to pick up their No.7 because it was one marker against one forward in those days.
> I knew on the day I was having a good game, because I was winning my 50-50s and I looked across at Bill Leivers, Roy Paul and Dave Ewing and they'd be winning theirs too."

7 because it was one marker against one forward in those days. I knew on the day I was having a good game, because I was winning my 50-50s and I looked across at Bill Leivers, Roy Paul and Dave Ewing and they'd be winning theirs too. It's a team game and we were all covering up for ourselves at the back. It was us against them and we fought for each other instinctively. If somebody got beat then someone else would go over and tackle that same player. We all knew if we played to the best of our ability, we should win because we were a better team than Birmingham and the Revie Plan was giving us such success over a short period of time because it was disrupting other teams."

City were very laid back and demonstrated an almost lazy manner. Birmingham were perplexed by this Hungarian-style play. Of course, this was the formation used by the magical Magyars in their 6-3 win at Wembley in 1953. Joe Hayes' early left-foot volley settled any lingering nerves before Kinsey equalised, leaving the score even at the interval.

Revie, who had set up Hayes in the first half, then turned provider for Jackie Dyson and it was 2-1. A minute later, Scottish genius Bobby Johnstone made the game safe. Revie had been omitted from the '55 team, to much criticism from journalists and fans alike and only featured in '56 because of an injury to Bill Spurdle on the morning of the game. Yet this final was later christened the 'Revie Final'.

Of course, the '56 final will always been remembered for Bert Trautmann playing the last 15 minutes with a broken neck - although the scale of his injury wasn't known at the time. After a collision with Murphy of Birmingham, Bert lay on the floor. Dave Ewing cleared the ball out of play and Roy takes up the story. "When he made his sensational dive at Murphy's feet there was no yelp of pain from Bert, although there was later on when Roy Paul slapped him on the back in celebration! Lawrie Barnett, the coach, was saying to him, 'Can you continue, Bert? Are you sure?' I had a feeling they were going to ask me to go in net so I started moving away, just in case! Even when we re-started, I still thought they'd put me in for some reason."

Roy was ecstatic when the final whistle blew. He'd buried the memory of that early goal by Jackie Milburn once and for all. "I'm very lucky. I had a good career, but how many other people can say they've got an FA Cup Winners' medal? We made a lot of people very happy and when you look through that team - Bert cost nothing. Bill Leivers cost nothing. I cost nothing. Roy Paul cost nothing. Dave Ewing, Joe Hayes, Ken Barnes and Bill Spurdle all cost nothing. Bobby Johnstone and Roy Clarke cost a few thousands from Hibs and Cardiff respectively. Don Revie cost 40 odd thousand pounds. I'm not knocking players nowadays because you can't compare different eras but I wonder how many of them are proud to put that bloody blue shirt on? Do they out it on because it's there to be put on? Or do they look at it and think 'here we go, here we go, down the tunnel and away you go'. You're more likely to get loyalty out of an English lad and especially a local Mancunian lad than you would from somebody transferred from somewhere else. As I say, I went onto play for Brighton and Crystal Palace but I never had the same passion for them as I did for Manchester City. I was proud and privileged to wear that blue shirt. Pride of my life that."

TOMMY BOOTH
22ND MARCH 1969
FA CUP SEMI-FINAL
EVERTON 0 CITY 1
ATT: 63,020

There's nothing Manchester City fans love more than seeing one of their own making their mark in the first team. One such player, who performed at the highest level with great distinction throughout the 1970s, was Thomas Anthony Booth. The local lad made good won honour after honour during a glorious spell during City's halcyon era. Although Tommy was too young to feature in City's famous Championship winning year of 1968, he broke into the first team after the disappointing home draw with Fenerbahçe in the European Cup. The lad who was born to play for City never looked back.

After seizing his opportunity and holding down his place he went on to write himself into Manchester City folklore. He gained an FA Cup Winners' medal and two League Cup winners' medals, together with one runners-up medal from 1974, a European Cup Winners' Cup medal and a Charity Shield appearance together with a League Championship runners-up medal in 1977. Tommy also gained four England Under-23 caps and was called up to the full England squad.

However, for all the glory of the countless finals and for all the pride of playing with those three lions on his chest, Tommy greatest thrill wasn't one of these games. Tommy's best memory was the 1969 FA Cup semi-final at Villa Park where, thanks to Tommy's late, late winner, the Blues booked a place in the Wembley Final, where they went onto defeat already-relegated Leicester City by a goal to nil.

Tommy was born to play for City. A staunch Blue as

a schoolboy, Tommy grew up kicking a ball from the age of four in the side streets off Queens Road in New Moston, before the family moved onto the Langley estate, another blue area on the edge of Middleton. So when City signed him, did they know they were signing a boyhood fan?

"Yes they did," says Tommy, "my dad was also called Tommy and he was friends with City's legendary chief scout, Harry Godwin. One day when I was four or five Harry saw me kicking a ball around and doing a few tricks. He must have been impressed for he said to my dad, 'Keep an eye on this one, Tommy, as soon as he's old enough we'll have him signed up!' and funnily enough that's exactly what happened. I was a City lad through and through and I was dead chuffed. I was still living at me mum and dad's and it was just a dream come true.

OPPOSITE: Tommy's career spanned two great eras at Maine Road, helping City reach Wembley in the sixties, seventies and eighties.

"So that was back in 1965 when I signed apprentice forms and you had to make your way through the old 'A' and 'B' teams before you could get to the first team. Seeing what was happening around the club with Joe and Malcolm turning things around and also with me being a local lad, it just made me so determined to be part of it down at City and stay the course. Funnily enough, my dad, who up until then had been so supportive of my football career, all of a sudden had reservations and wanted me to finish my apprenticeship with a local company, Mather and Platt! But here I was with the chance to make the grade with City and luckily everything clicked into place."

Tommy signed from apprentice on 26th August 1967. He'd captained City's youth teams and now waited patiently on the sidelines as his heroes enjoyed a season of unprecedented success. Manchester City were League Champions. It would surely take some player to break into this team, but Tommy did just that, becoming the great discovery of the 1968-

69 season. In retrospect, the title triumph of 1968 seemed a short-lived affair. Much was made of the fact that they were tipped to do well in the European Cup, with a famous quote from Malcolm Allison eventually coming back to haunt him.

"The Fenerbahçe game was a major blow to the club. People know these days what it's like over there now, but at the time it was a new thing, we were all taken by surprise. I wasn't even playing but I felt intimidated just watching it all from the sidelines. I was 18 or 19, I'd never even been abroad before! Of course, Malcolm had turned round and said, 'We'll terrify Europe' and we promptly got knocked out in the first round! Then we won the European Cup Winners' Cup the following year which is when Allison said, 'I always said we'd terrify Europe, I never said which year though!'

"The start of the title defence hadn't begun too well and then we were dumped out of Europe in the first week of October. They were hammer blows to the club. Then again, it was because of that start and the early exit that I finally got my chance. You know, you're sat on the sidelines wanting the team to do well and I never ever wanted us to lose just because it might give me a chance to play."

City thrashed West Bromwich Albion 6-1 in the

Charity Shield. All seemed well for another season of domination. The defence began with a 2-1 defeat at Liverpool, but then City recorded their first win of the season - 3-2 against Wolves. The next match was the game all of Manchester had been waiting for - champions of England, Manchester City against champions of Europe, Manchester United. It ended 0-0 but from there City's form took an alarming nosedive. Heavy defeats at Leicester and Arsenal interspersed with uninspiring draws with QPR and Ipswich meant Joe Mercer handing a first team jersey to the young man from North Manchester.

"It was a fantastic feeling to finally get my debut in a City shirt. It was what I had worked towards all the time. My debut was in the League Cup at Huddersfield Town, I think we drew that game and then it was a tough baptism of fire in the league, we played Arsenal on the Wednesday night and Tottenham three days later. I think we beat them 4-0, they had Greaves and Gilzean playing amongst others and even Arsenal were building their double-winning squad, so as you can imagine, I'm playing against high calibre professionals and my confidence started to soar.

"The Fenerbahçe game was a major blow to the club. People know these days what it's like over there now, but at the time it was a new thing, we were all taken by surprise. I wasn't even playing but I felt intimidated just watching it all from the sidelines."

"Overall the Championship form wasn't too clever and we were out of the race early on so the FA Cup became our season. It was our last real chance to win anything that year and we all started to get a feeling that a Cup run was a possibility. The farther we got in the competition, the more pressure we were under to deliver the goods and rescue the season. We didn't want to lose the momentum gained over the last three seasons and we had to give the fans something back, as well as shutting up our critics."

It is worth noting here that Tommy's

view was that City were determined not to lose the momentum they'd previously gained. This would have been his mindset at the time. Yet Tommy was not an old pro, he was the youngest member of the squad and here he was leading by example, displaying all the mental toughness and drive required to succeed at the top level. He wasn't hiding behind the older players. In fact he was becoming as respected as any of them in almost no time at all.

The line-up for his league debut against Arsenal read: Dowd; Connor, Pardoe; Doyle, Booth, Oakes; Lee, Bell, Summerbee, Young and Coleman. In no time at all, Tommy became a City regular, displacing big George Heslop at the heart of City's defence, a role he enjoyed alongside Mike Doyle until the emergence of Dave Watson when Tommy became a holding midfield player. Yet Tommy's personal Blue heaven came on Saturday 22nd March 1969. The Blues had already beaten Luton Town, Newcastle United and Blackburn Rovers to reach the sixth round where a solitary Francis Lee strike was enough to see off Tottenham.

Already they had gone one better than in 1967 when, after playing Leeds off the park at Elland Road, City lost in the quarter-finals to a controversial Jack Charlton goal. So everything was set-up for the semi-final, the venue Villa Park, where City had won in the 1956 semi-final. Younger readers may be surprised to learn that kick-off times for these big games were always at 3pm on a Saturday afternoon!

Tommy takes up the tale. "The day before the semi-final we went away to Matlock, just to have a change of scenery and to release some of the pressure. Matlock was very picturesque, very beautiful and it helped take our mind off things. We were all taking the mickey out of each other as usual beforehand and the banter was flying around, but an hour or two before the game, the atmosphere become a lot more subdued.

"I sensed a feeling around the dresing room that this was a serious chance. We really realised what was at stake and we all thought, 'we can't lose this one'. Of course, someone's got to lose, there's got to be a winner, there's got to be a loser but we all just hoped it wasn't going to be us. We so desperately wanted to put it together on the day like we knew we could and come out on top."

The stakes were huge. There was a chance to repair what had been an indifferent campaign by Joe Mercer's high standards. City were 90 minutes away from Wembley. As the teams ran out, City's huge following in the Holte End made their presence felt. They needed to as well as on the pitch City faced a formidable obstacle in Cup holders Everton.

"Going into the semi, the bookies made Everton slight favourites. They had some tough players and we knew it was going to be a battle," says Tommy.

Everton's midfield dynamo Alan Ball was marked out of the game by Dave Connor and the match itself was a stalemate for long periods. One thing though, was spurring Tommy Booth on.

"Looking out at all our fans, I wanted to win just for them. For ourselves of course, but we were playing for those magnificent supporters too. They played their part on the day, because from what I can remember it was a really hard game. I say from what I remember, because in all fairness, I don't recall too much of the actual game.

"Fans who were there point out things about the game: 'Remember when you did this Tommy, remember when you did that?' and I can't visualise them because I'd have been focusing so much on the man in front of me. What we were aware of is that it was late in the game. People in the stands had already started to leave and you could see the odd gap appearing in the seats. Of course, there was no extra time in those days, so it would've meant a replay after the 90 minutes were up.

"Neil Young got through on goal and the Everton keeper, Gordon West, made a great save at his near post. We all looked around at each other and shrugged because we felt that late in the game that was probably our best chance gone, but we were all waved forward for the ensuing corner which Youngy took himself. He floated it into the near post and Mike Summerbee nodded it across goal. It came to me and I stuck it in with my left foot from close range. Well, I can't tell you what a feeling that was. I ran over to the City fans behind the goal who were going absolutely beserk.

"At that moment all the pressure of the game was lifted from my shoulders. It didn't last long because a moment later, I felt another pressure on my shoulders as the whole team converged on top of me! We'd done it. We'd made it to the Final and we knew we could beat Leicester City and win the Cup.

"If you lose in a semi-final, no-one remembers you. But if lose in a final, at least you get to that final and experience playing at Wembley. You get the day out and all that goes with it. And for me, a local lad, 19 years of age playing in my first season, to score such an important goal in the history of the club, in the very last minute of a tense game, well that's unbelievable. Roy of the Rovers stuff. My first-ever goal. What a time and place to score it! I was so proud. I get goose pimples and shivers down my spine just

BELOW: Tommy takes command of the situation again, this time watched by 'King' Colin.

171

ABOVE:
Tommy scores
the winner
in the 1969
FA Cup
semi final
- Tommy's
first goal as a
professional.

telling you all this now. The hairs on the back of my neck are standing up just speaking about it."

City's genial manager Joe Mercer heaped praise on his young gun Tommy. He talked him up in the press as the best footballing centre half since Stan Cullis. To his team-mates, he was simply 'Chalky', the Mancunian who had put the Blues in sight of the Twin Towers.

"Afterwards the atmosphere amongst the lads was electric. The coach journey home was fantastic. We went back to Matlock to continue the celebrations and I can tell you, we were absolutely legless that night. God, we put some drink away, I got home about four in the morning absolutely steaming and my mother went ballistic at me for waking the whole house up!

"So we'd rescued the season for the club. We were in the FA Cup Final and of course the game was watched worldwide even then. The FA Cup is one of the world's most coveted pieces of silverware, a classic all-time trophy and even now if I visit schools, the City fans want to see the FA Cup winners' medal more than any of the others.

"We were all looking forward to the final, we were all feeling supremely confident and although we won the Cup by just one goal we brought it home to 300,000 people in Manchester. By doing that we had also booked an early return to European competition, which of course we later terrified properly! After the cup was won we had more celebrations in the hotel with all the wives and girlfriends and then went onto the Cafe Royale for a party!"

Of course, Tommy notched another important cup goal, at Peterborough in the '81 cup run and although he was part of the squad in '81 and was named on the bench, it is the '69 cup run which remains so special to him. He's scored other important league goals, 26 in all for City during his 14 years at the club as a professional, but none can find a place in his heart like that one at Villa Park.

These days Tommy is a regular at the City of Manchester Stadium. He also attends a number of City supporters' meetings, where he always receives a thunderous reception. "Whenever I see the fans at these functions, and I attend quite a few these days, they all come up to me and say, 'I was there Tommy, I was there at the semi when you scored the winner', and that means so much to me. They ask you to bring along your medals and talk about the games you played in. There's the older fans, so knowledgeable and the younger ones, so passionate but they've not seen the glory, well not yet anyway. I long for City to be truly successful again so that these fans are rewarded for their loyalty."

UWE ROSLER
18ᵀᴴ FEBRUARY 1996
FA CUP FIFTH ROUND
MANCHESTER UNITED 2 CITY 1
ATT 42,692

There cannot have been many City players more idolised over the years than 'Der Bomber', otherwise known as Uwe Rosler. Legend has it that his granddad dropped a bomb on Old Trafford during a Luftwaffe mission over Manchester during the war! This is total cobblers of course but the story helped to make him a true cult hero during his five seasons at the club. His goals, industry and wholehearted commitment to the cause endeared him greatly to the support. And although Uwe left City under something of a cloud back in 1998, at a time when the Blue Army were contemplating the possibility of a league derby with Macclesfield Town, such is the popularity of Uwe Rosler that his name is still sung as loudly at the home matches as it was back in the days of Brian Horton, Frank Clark and Alan Ball.

Most City fans didn't have a clue who Rosler was when he arrived in Moss Side back in 1994 but at the time The Blues were short of goals. After a 4-0 hammering at Coventry, the writing looked to be on the wall and inspiration was required as a matter of urgency. A fee of £300,000 secured the signature of the prolific FC Nuremburg striker and though he was unknown to us had he heard of City.

"Well, the name of Manchester City is well known in Germany and I knew they'd beaten Schalke when they were at their peak. I also knew of the German connection with Bert Trautmann. Actually I've only met Bert a couple of times but I know how the City fans took to him and after all I've been through, I can relate to his experiences a little because they took to

174

me too and I'm eternally grateful for that. So yes, I'd heard of Manchester City but I've got to be honest, I knew nothing of their recent history, or of the current set-up. I didn't know who they had on their books at the time."

Rosler made his debut at QPR, a game in which David Rocastle scored his last-ever goal for the Blues. Towards the end of that season Rosler found his scoring boots and chipped in with some vital goals. By the time he scored City's equaliser in the last game of the season at Hillsborough, the travelling army of 9,500 were chanting "Uwe, Uwe Rosler" to the tune of *Go West*. It was to be his anthem during his stay at the club. His trademark celebration was to bend on one knee and wiggle his arm in and out, less specatular than Beagrie's somersaults but seen more often.

Season 1994-95 saw the introduction of Nicky Summerbee and a widening of the hallowed Maine Road turf. It also saw the arrival of that best selling T-shirt 'Rosler's Granddad bombed Old Trafford'. Depicted on the shirt was a German plane dropping bombs with MCFC written on them. On the back of the shirt the date February 21st 1941 was provided as proof of historical accuracy. There is some doubt over the accuracy of this date however, the one thing that cannot be denied is that it was a cracking T-shirt and at a fiver a throw, they sold like hot cakes on the forecourt. "Even my son walks round in one at home," laughs Uwe, "I think it's a brilliant laugh!"

The opening day fixture in 1994-95 saw Uwe dismissed at Arsenal but an early season spell of goals saw Rosler continue where he'd left off before, his delicious lob over Southall in the 4-0 thrasing of Everton the pick of that early bunch. With Rosler doing so well in the goalscoring charts and with Germany's World Cup exit to Bulgaria fresh in the mind, the clamour for Uwe to be called up to the full national side began in earnest.

"I played up front for East Germany in the old days when it was West and East. We had a great side, there was Thomas Doll, Karl Heinz Riedle, Andreas Thom and Matthaus Sammer. I also had experience of European football with Dynamo Dresden so I felt if the call came that I'd be equipped to play for the reunified side. I missed the City - Tottenham game, the famous 5-2, and I think the fans believed that might have hindered my chances of getting that cap because had I played it would have been billed as Rosler v Klinsmann and it would have meant a chance to shine in direct comparison. However Berti Vogts was aware of me regardless. I was very close to a full call-up. They were watching me all the time during my time in the Premiership, they knew exactly where I was and knew exactly what I could do. I was invited to a training camp and given encouragement. I also played in a tribute game for Guido Buchwald the famous VFB Stuttgart and Germany defender along with most of the current German squad. In any case I scored in the return fixture down at White Hart Lane."

Uwe and the City fans waited for the call that never came. Even though City's league form was deteriorating alarmingly, Rosler's winner at Ipswich had briefly lifted City to the dizzy heights of sixth in December. Uwe kept on scoring and his goals were to prove the difference between staying up and relegation. Four at home in the League Cup against Notts County stand out

176

in the memory as does the equaliser at Newcastle in the FA Cup tie, together with an extravagant shirt-twirling celebration. The 2-0 League Cup win at Newcastle and the vital 3-2 victory over Blackburn at Ewood Park were also special games. Uwe notched his 20th league goal at Villa, an admirable feat in a struggling side. By the start of the next season, 1995-96, Rosler had already become talisman-in-chief at Maine Road.

Yet in the wake of Brian Horton's departure came a period of uncertainty, followed by Francis Lee's incredible decision to appoint Alan Ball as club manager. Soon after, Rosler's strike partner and soul mate Paul Walsh was sold to Portsmouth, leaving Rosler with Niall Quinn and Gerry Creaney to feed off the scraps from Nigel Clough and Martin 'Buster' Phillips, who Ball had foolishly labelled "the next £10m player." It was to prove to be a long hard winter.

RIGHT: Cult hero Rosler was provided moments of rare pride for City during the grim 90s.

"I said at the time that what we were doing was all wrong. I said we couldn't hope to get out of the relegation battles and the lower leagues if we were resorting to buying players who were sat on the bench at clubs further down the league than ourselves. If they're not good enough for that club, they shouldn't be good enough for Manchester City. We let a lot of good players go and replaced them with inferior ones. Each time a new manager came in, he'd want to sign three or four new players which is understandable, but then another manager would come in and do the same and eventually we had about 54 professionals on the books!"

City's league form saw the club suffer the brunt of some cruel jokes - mostly involving the fact that a triangle could boast three points, something City couldn't until November. A 6-0 thumping at Liverpool saw Rosler launch his boots into the congregation of visiting Mancunians in the Anfield Road end, a gesture widely misrepresented by the press as a sign that Rosler was leaving the club. He was merely looking for some luckier boots.

At least the FA Cup was providing something of a welcome distraction. A goalless draw at Leicester meant a replay and the 5-0 win that it produced was amazing in that City hadn't scored more than one goal in a league game until New Year's Day. It was amazing also to think that Leicester boss Martin O'Neill was under real pressure to deliver at that stage.

Round four sent City to Coventry but the original tie was postponed because of bad weather. By the time the rearranged game had taken place, the City supporters already knew their potential opponents in the fifth round - Manchester United.

The final whistle in the 2-2 draw at Highfield Road was blown just as Uwe broke through on goal but City won the replay 2-1, just days before the fifth round tie. It meant the game all of Manchester was waiting for was on. The queue for derby tickets formed almost immediately after the game.

"My favourite memory was the cup-tie at Old Trafford where we lost 2-1 against United. You may be surprised by that choice, after all it's no fun losing in a derby at any time, least of all one so high-profile and with us, even then, chasing that elusive piece of silverware. For me, though, it was a special occasion. We played in the league game earlier that season at United and they didn't give any tickets to City fans even though they already had a high capacity at their ground. On this occasion, we had 8,000 Blues behind the goal and they were making all the noise right throughout the game.

"We were up for this one, there was a real buzz in the city all week and for this afternoon we could forget about our league form. We felt that having so many City fans in the ground would give us a lift and everything was going so well up until the penalty. The atmosphere that day was absolutely awesome."

On 12 minutes a through ball from Kinkladze found Rosler who had timed his run to perfection. He was bearing down on goal and the stadium held its breath.

"For me it was a great goal to score in a great stadium against a great team and because of these factors I would say it's my all-time favourite City goal. I scored with a cracking volley from 30 metres in a game back in Germany years ago but with this one Schmeichel was coming out so I had to make a snap decision as to what I should do next? Should I take it round him? Or carry it on into the box? He raced out quite quickly to close down the angle so in the end I just lobbed him and it seemed an eternity before the ball dropped in - but it looked a goal from the moment it left my foot. I was so proud when I scored, I ran straight over to the City supporters who were doing their best to join me and the players in a big hug! So at 1-0 we were doing okay, the game plan was working and although it may seem like a harsh thing to say but my German friend Michael Frontzeck made a mistake that afternoon.

"You've got to be streetwise when you go to that ground and you tend to get very little from the referee. He did have hold of the player's shirt so technically it was a foul. The inconsistency with this rule is a real problem, you see far worse go on in the box but nothing is ever given, so to be penalised for this offence just when we were taking the sting out of their game was a tough thing to have to accept. It was a silly thing for Michael to do though because it gave the referee an opportunity to

> "I said at the time that what we were doing was all wrong. I said we couldn't hope to get out of the relegation battles and the lower leagues if we were resorting to buying players who were sat on the bench at clubs further down the league than ourselves. If they're not good enough for that club, they shouldn't be good enough for Manchester City."

make a ruling and that gave United a chance to get back into the game.

"All the City players chased the referee but he shouldn't have given the referee that chance to penalise us. It changed the game. I'm not saying we would have won but we were sitting back, hitting them on the break and looking for the killer second goal. I certainly don't think we'd have lost.

"The ball had cleared his head from the corner and was going away from goal. He wasn't even facing goal and he [Frontzeck] made a challenge that was unnecessary. Yes, it was extremely harsh but we spoke about keeping our discipline before the game."

After the cup exit just one target remained: to avoid relegation. With the Sky TV deal to be renegotiated at the end of the season the gulf between the Premiership and the Football League clubs would become wider than ever. City's run-in was difficult. Rosler scored in the 3-3 draw with Newcastle, a game notorious for Faustino Asprilla's disgusting elbow on Keith Curle, an assault that went unpunished by referee Martin Bodenham. Rosler looked to have rescued a point for City in the next derby in April when he turned Pallister inside out and drove a low shot past Schmeichel. He gesticulated to manager Alan Ball and pointed out the name on the back of his shirt. He wasn't dropped again. The nervous climax to the season saw City gain two late wins over Sheffield Wednesday and Aston Villa. But these wins were matched by Coventry and Southampton. Rosler scored a penalty against Liverpool on the final day, when Stevie Lomas was told to keep the ball in the corner to run down the clock. City were relegated.

"When we went down Berti Vogts phoned me and said, 'You have to leave City if you want to play for Germany.' He said he wouldn't consider anyone who didn't play in the top league. I said, 'No. No way. I love City and I'm staying here.' It was then and only then that my international chances were put to rest."

At the start of the following season Alan Ball was dismissed shortly after the Stoke game and City then had another managerless spell, the second in five years, before they could secure another manager. The fans who travelled to Crystal Palace chanted 'Nobody's Blue and White Army' as George Graham and then Dave Bassett turned down the job.

"I don't wish to say anything too political because it's been and gone and City are now moving forward again. At the time though, I couldn't understand it why people were turning the job down. In my eyes Manchester City were, are and always will be a big and important club. Whether it was because funds were short or maybe they were put off having a working relationship with Francis Lee - I don't know.

"I know a lot of City fans wanted the chairman out in the end but he never got on my back once. His son, Gary Lee, is one of my closest friends, a friend for life. He helped me settle in England and found me accommodation at a time when I couldn't speak the language very well. So from a personal point of view, I was quite content had Francis Lee stayed on as chairman! Frank Clark too, I got on well with him and we shook hands on a deal, a new four-year contract. He told me to go on holiday and we'd sort it out when we came back, but when I returned Joe Royle had come in and it was then and only then that I started to look for a new club."

Rosler forged a partnership with Paul Dickov and later Lee Bradbury. While Dickov passed into City legend with his goal at Wembley, Bradbury struggled to score in a team falling apart at the seams.

"I felt really sorry for Lee. He was a good lad and the amount of money that City paid for him was too much, considering that he had one played one full year in the First Division. He fell under the weight of expectation and you could see his head dropping on

the pitch. You could see him dropping deeper and deeper to get a touch of the ball and get involved."

As City fell into the ignominy of the Second Division, Kinkladze and Rosler headed for the Champions League, with Ajax and Kaiserslautern respectively. After moving to Norway to play for Oslo outfit Lillestrom, disaster struck once more. Time didn't so much stand still, more Uwe's life flashed before his eyes. The brave German had to fight one more battle. He was diagnosed with chest cancer. It was a battle which meant everything else in his life was to go on hold. Uwe told the press that he and his family would need to be left alone for the next few months.

Immediately, City website BlueView set up a message board for fans to pass on their regards to Uwe Rosler. The City supporters chanted his name in the last three home games of the 2002-03 season.

"They have always supported me, the City fans. I don't know why they like me so much, maybe it's because I bought all the beer that night in the nightclub in the Isle of Man! They're an extension of my family though and they have played their part in lifting my spirits during some hard and very painful times. I found it very hard to come to terms with the news and very early on I was in hospital in real pain after going through a bout of tough chemotherapy. I felt ill, I felt helpless and then they brought in over 1,000 emails from City fans for me to read. You cannot imagine how important those emails are. You can't believe how much hope that gave me. They said 'Come on Uwe, you are a fighter, you will win', and it helped me fight it. I immediately thought, 'Yes, you can win this battle Uwe'.

"Whenever I felt in pain, whenever it was getting all too much, I'd get out these emails and re-read every single one of them. I will never throw any of them away. They will stay with me till the day I die. In my mind, I have imagined coming back, walking out to say thankyou to the City fans. I know Bernard Halford has invited me and Paul Walsh to walk onto the pitch before a home game but I'm only going to come here when I'm absolutely 100% cured. I have promised myself that I can only do this when I know I will live for sure."

Who knows what the future hold for Uwe Rosler? He said in a magazine interview he wanted to become Manchester City manager one day in the future. If he doesn't fulfill all his dreams, then it won't be as important now, just so long as he is happy and healthy. The love affair between Uwe and his fans will go on and on.

bobby murdoch, different class
by david potter
foreword by billy mcneill
£10.99 - 344pp - 16pp photographs

David W. Potter's biography of one of Celtic's greatest players, is a celebration of the era and the man. The 1960s represented the dawn of a new era for Britain in general and Glasgow in particular, while Potter's prose sings with the delight of being around at the time. As the author says of the period, to borrow a line from Wordsworth's celebration of the French Revolution of 1789;

**'Bliss it was in that dawn to be alive,
But to be young was very heaven!'**

THE TWO FACES OF
LEE HARVEY
OSWALD

A TALE OF DECEPTION, BETRAYAL AND MURDER
BY GLENN B FLEMING
£8.99 - 355pp

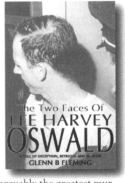

Of all the millions of words written in anger or certainty regarding arguably the greatest murder mystery of all time, the assassination of President John Fitzgerald Kennedy, one testimony remains glaringly absent. The deposition of Lee Harvey Oswald, the alleged assassin, was silenced by Jack Ruby's bullet before he could tell his story to a shocked and grieving world.

The Two Faces of Lee Harvey Oswald is a unique work. No other book in the public domain concentrates on Lee Oswald's point of view; a young man caught up by, then hopelessly trapped in, history.

From the moment of his return from the Soviet Union, Oswald became tangled in a web of intrigue, deception and murder. And yet, no amount of speculation or rumour mongering can lend history in general and Oswald in particular, his own words.

"I'm just a patsy!" Oswald screamed, as he was led along a corridor in the Dallas Police Building, shortly after his arrest that fateful weekend. We will never truly know how innocent, or guilty, Oswald was. But his memory deserves a hearing. The most accurate hearing possible.

Order by Credit Card 0161 872 3319

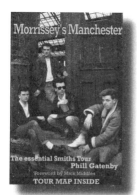

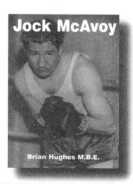